CHRISTIANS

AND

THE THEATER.

BY J. M. BUCKLEY.

"Prove all things, hold fast that which is good."

NEW YORK:
NELSON & PHILLIPS.
CINCINNATI:
HITCHCOCK & WALDEN.
1876.

PREFACE.

IT was my desire to write a book on the Theater in its relation to Christian sentiment and conduct, in which every idea should be pertinent to the subject in hand, and from which nothing vital to its just treatment should be omitted.

I intended that every statement made therein should be true, either of matters of history or in the description of existing facts and institutions.

I wished the whole to be written in language colloquial yet correct, and without diffuseness or repetition.

It was also in my plan that the treatise should be so brief that it could be *read aloud* without haste, and discussed at home, or in schools, or in teachers' meetings, in one or two evenings.

That these hopes have become realities I cannot flatter myself until my attempt shall have undergone the charitable scrutiny of friends, and until the keen eye and keener dart of hostile criticism shall have done their work upon it. But with respect to the element of brevity I am sure that the purpose avowed has been attained.

CONTENTS.

CHRISTIANS AND THE THEATER.

CHAPTER I.

INTRODUCTORY.

THE Theater is an institution which has existed for many hundreds of years, traces of it being found a thousand years before Christ. Probably never in its history, in Europe and this country, was it, viewed in all its bearings, more flourishing than it is at the present time. Not that the present is a period distinguished by the production of plays of remarkable excellence, for the contrary is true; or that there are many actors of the first reputation, or more than one or two who compare favorably with the brilliant names of a former generation. But in the number of its patrons, the amount of its financial receipts, and the extent of its hold upon the country at large, the Theatre has never been more successful than it is now. Not only is it thoroughly established in the large cities, where it has always prospered; but in "provincial" places large halls and "opera" houses have been erected, and theatrical companies, made up for the tour, perform throughout the entire country; and even in out-of-the-way villages a "superannuated" "star," supported by a dilapidated "cast," may be found delighting the rustics, and impressing them with the belief that they have in him a worthy rival of Garrick, or, at least, of the most distinguished actors of the day. When persons from the country visit any of our larger cities, they not unfrequently, unless restrained by religious considerations, propose to attend the Theater, although at home, where well known, they would conscientiously abstain from such recreation. The number of persons of, in general, strict views, who visit this institution more or less frequently, is larger now than it has been for many years, perhaps than it has ever been in this country.

The Theater is largely, though indirectly, connected with general literature; sentences, peculiar turns of expression, apothegms in particular plays which strike the public fancy, become incorporated with the conversation and newspaper and magazine articles of the day; while many of the larger periodicals present discussions of plays, *critiques* of actors, etc.; and the daily papers give to the community every morning a column or two of criticism on the performances of the preceding evening, written, in many instances, with so much discrimination and in such an attractive manner as to make very interesting reading. Under these circumstances the position proper to be taken by Christians toward the Theater is much debated in almost every household. Individual Christians have to determine what it is right for them to do, and parents, guardians, and educators are obliged to decide what they may encourage or allow to those in their charge.

To whatever conclusion the conscientious Christian may come, he who assists him in the solution of the problem by a careful presentation of the subject in all its relations, will perform a real service. Believing that there is a place, and that there is a positive demand for such a discussion as will bear the test of a rigorous examination of the principles maintained, the author submits the following chapters as the best contribution which he can make to the elucidation of this theme.

CHAPTER II.

HOW THE THEATER IS REGARDED BY THE ROMAN CATHOLIC AND GREEK CHURCHES.

THE Roman Catholic Church, notwithstanding the blows which it has received from Mohammedanism, and more recently from the great Reformation and spread of Rationalism, is still the Church of Italy, Austria, France, Belgium, Spain, Portugal, Mexico, and South America, and is the controlling religious influence in Ireland, while it is very active in England and flourishing in the United States. As upon many subjects it is most pronounced, and on some questions has never sought to conciliate adverse opinion, it is worth while to consider its treatment of theatrical amusements. In its ritual it makes more use of dramatic representation than any other body bearing the Christian name, and in some parts of the world, at certain seasons, actually dramatizes the scenes of the crucifixion. To ordinary theatrical amusements it is tolerant, and in the countries which are exclusively Catholic they are allowed and patronized without rebuke, by the population generally. In most or all of these countries the Theaters are open on Sunday evenings, when the most popular plays are put upon the boards and are witnessed by larger concourses than usual. But in Lent the people are dissuaded, and in fact prohibited, from going, and those who are at all devotional, or recognize the authority of the Church, either abstain wholly from plays, or studiously avoid the more frivolous, attending only on tragedies. In some countries, where the civil law is controlled by the Church of Rome, the Theaters are closed in Lent. It is a fact, however, of some interest and significance, that with few exceptions, if any, those "orders" and individuals who lay claim to peculiar devotion renounce theatrical amusements altogether. But they pursue the same course with regard to other amusements, and place abstinence from them on the same ground on which they rest the obligation of fasting, vigils, additional prayers, masses, and divers forms of self-denial and voluntary humiliation. While the average Catholic population are allowed to attend the Theaters, except at certain seasons, and are countenanced by the presence of their priests in so doing, many bishops, priests, and monks have strongly condemned theatrical amusements, and written weighty arguments against them, some going so far as to declare that they are "instruments of Satan," "a curse to the Church," "beguiling unstable souls;" and charging those priests who lend those amusements their influence with leading the flock of God astray. I have been told, on good authority, that there have been papal allocutions against Theaters; but, however this may be, with the exceptions above-named, the spirit of the Romish Church has been one of tolerance, if not of friendship, toward them.

The Greek Church, "predominating in all Russia, European Turkey, Greece, the Ionian Isles, and Montenegro," holds about the same relation to the Theater which characterizes the Church of Rome, and has not thought it important to instruct its people on the subject, at least to any extent perceptible to the outside world.

CHAPTER III.

THE THEATER AND THE PROTESTANT CHURCHES.

THE results of the Lutheran Reformation, direct and indirect, to the Christian world can never be fully estimated, for they must continue and extend to the end of time. No denomination is what it would have been without that Reformation; perhaps no individual Christian is what he would have been without it. Rapidly spreading over Germany, Sweden, Norway, and Denmark, it did not work any great change in the views or practices of the people of those countries with regard to the observance of the Sabbath, or the question of amusements.

It is now generally conceded that the change, as far as it related to the external life of the communities which it affected, was more nearly nominal than, until comparatively recently, it was supposed to have been. The authority of the pope was shaken off, masses, confessions, absolutions, monkish orders, and the spurious sacraments were abolished; but in other respects the greater part of the people went on as they had done. The doctrine of justification by faith was preached, and the corresponding duty of consecrating the heart and life to God was enforced, but it was a long time before any great and general change in religious experience took place. And, in truth, the spirit of rationalism soon appeared, so that three or more parties arose, one evangelical and devout, another critical and semi-skeptical, and a third simply ritualistic. For the most part the subject of amusements was left to the people, and "every man did what was right in his own eyes." Theatrical amusements flourish in these countries and are seldom denounced, though many ministers and laymen in communion with the State Church exert a powerful influence in favor of a discrimination based on the necessities of a religious experience.

In Switzerland, especially in Geneva, very different views prevailed. During the twenty-three years of Calvin's rule no public amusements were permitted, and the gamester was "pilloried with a pack of cards around his neck." Theatrical performances were interdicted by one of Calvin's laws, which remained unrepealed for more than two centuries after his death. As late as the time of Voltaire the prejudices of the citizens were against plays, but now "the Salle de Spectacle can be seen close to the Porte Neuve," and the population frequent the Theater on Sabbath more than on any other day. In most, if not in all of the cantons, the Theater is allowed, and the people, except the more strictly religious, as in Germany or France, patronize it as often as they wish.

In England the Reformation affected the manners of the people even less than in Germany. Henry VIII., as head of the Church, was not in a condition to promote good morals, and the issue on which he broke with the pope did not at all strengthen his spiritual influence. The return of Romanism under Mary, the partial reformation under Elizabeth, and the subsequent struggles, left the mass of the people to do as they pleased; and intemperance, Sabbath-breaking, gaming, and all kinds of dissipation, were prevalent. The authority of the priests and the confessional having been destroyed, and no great moral force substituted, the bulk of the population differed but little from the people of Catholic countries. To this day the Theater is, in general, popular among the communicants of the English Church, subject to the restrictions in Lent; with the exception of many of the more strict clergymen and of a few bishops, who, supported by a small proportion of laymen, do not favor any of the amusements known as "worldly."

In Scotland, however, the Reformation was principally promoted and organized by John Knox, and men of like stamp. Knox, when driven out of the country, spent two years with Calvin in Geneva, where he was established in his doctrines, principles, and views of morals, by the great learning, vast ability, indomitable will, and perseverance of that, in many respects, unparalleled man. Returning to Scotland, Knox laid the foundations of as rigid an adherence to doctrine, and as austere a morality, as have ever been seen in the history of Christianity. And by that morality Theaters were absolutely and irrevocably condemned, and those who attended them considered to be in the "gall of bitterness and the bond of iniquity."

CHAPTER IV.

THE THEATER AND THE PROTESTANT CHURCHES—CONTINUED.

THE sentiments and practices of the leading sects of Protestantism which have originated outside of, or split off from, the Churches of the Reformation, must now be considered.

The Presbyterians, under the legitimate operation of the Protestant principle and their anomalous relation to the State, have subdivided into various sects, and owing to the peculiar tendencies of the Scotch mind, so clear, penetrating, and tenacious, and, as one of its most distinguished American representatives has said, "as ready to die for a pin as for a post," have examined and argued every question at great length; but in all their divisions they are a unit in denouncing the Theater.

The Puritans and Independents, of every school, were equally decided in their opposition, and the early settlers of Massachusetts would have been as much shocked at the proposal to erect a Theater in Boston as they would have been at a movement to allow business and travel to proceed on the Lord's day.

The Congregationalists, in general, are still opposed to the Theater, though there is a growing tendency to relax among them, which is a cause of rejoicing to some and of alarm to others, according to the view which they take of the main question.

The Baptist denomination, in its many branches, now numbering more than the Presbyterians and Congregationalists united, has never had any sympathy with the Theater; and whatever certain individuals, ministers or laymen, in the great centers, may think or do, the spirit of the body is overwhelmingly against the institution.

The Society of Friends has, without exception, borne "testimony" against Theaters, as it has, indeed, against all diversion of every kind, even going so far as to condemn music, and to discipline its members for owning or using musical instruments, or allowing them in their homes.

The Protestant Episcopal Church in this country

has regarded the Theater in a light similar to that in which it is placed by the Church of England. To this may be added the remark, that the evangelical bishops and ministers of that Church are, perhaps, more pronounced in their opposition to attendance on public plays than their brethren in England, though there are, of course, individual exceptions of laxity in this country, and of strictness in England.

The Methodists in England and America were originally as rigid as the Friends, except that they did not condemn music, and as strenuous in enforcing their Discipline against fashionable amusements as were the Puritans or Calvin himself. Their rule forbidding "the taking such diversions as cannot be used in the name of the Lord Jesus" has from the beginning been understood to condemn and prohibit going to Theaters. Many, in the early history of the movement, were expelled under that rule for attending play-houses, and many deterred from joining these societies by the knowledge of the restriction.

But at all times, and in the strictest Churches, there have been some who, believing that the Theater ought not to be attended by Christians, have, nevertheless, indulged themselves therein, and suffered in their consciences for doing so. And there have always been some, both of the clergy and the laity, who have held that the opposition to the stage is not well founded and should be discontinued. Of these clergymen most, for the sake of peace, reputation, and influence, have kept their views to themselves, or communicated them privately to a few friends; while the laymen have been less deterred from acting in harmony with their sentiments.

At present the number of ministers in favor of a compromise between the Church and the Drama seems to be increasing in the cities, while many of the members of all Churches openly attend the Theater, some aiming to discriminate as to places and plays, but the many going where accident or fancy may lead them, while the immense majority of the sects originally condemning Theaters still hold their sentiments unchanged, and regard those who have departed as having fallen into serious errors of opinion and conduct.

CHAPTER V.

HOW THE THEATER IS DEFENDED.

IT is maintained by some that amusement is necessary, and that any amusement generally patronized by all classes of men, in all civilized countries, and for many ages, must meet a want of human nature. But what meets a want of human nature cannot be essentially evil, and, therefore, may be discriminatingly enjoyed. If these propositions, taken separately, are true, and the conclusions announced are properly drawn from them, the question is settled beyond room for doubt.

The first assertion "amusement is necessary," is almost self-evident. Asceticism may deny it, but the body and mind will alike rebel. The Theater has been generally patronized by most, if not all, classes of men, in all civilized countries, and for more than two thousand years. That it gratifies some of the desires of men, pleases their tastes, and powerfully attracts them, all must concede. The problem, however, is not solved by these facts until it shall be determined whether the desires which the Theater gratifies are, on the whole, such as the Christian should cherish and gratify, or such as, under the law of self-denial, are to be restricted or suppressed. If it be held that dramatic representation is not essentially evil, it would not follow that the *concrete* form in which it appears in a particular city or age could be justifiably encouraged. So that the summary way of disposing of the subject is not satisfactory. Others take the ground that the Theater exists, has existed, and will exist; that to denounce it is useless, and that Christians should address themselves to the work of pruning, reforming, and elevating it, rather than of assailing it in the spirit of narrowness and fanaticism.

That it exists, has existed, and will exist, is obvious; that to denounce it in the hope of destroying it, or preventing its financial success, is chimerical, is to every one, except a few enthusiasts, apparent; but that Christians are called upon to devote their energies to its reconstruction and purification would admit of considerable to be said on both sides. That it should not be assailed in the spirit of narrowness and fanaticism is certain, for that spirit cannot be defended in the plane either of reason or religion. Whether it should be assailed at all depends upon its nature and influence, and if these do not deserve condemnation, it should at least be let alone; and if they are not to be justified, a temperate and truthful exposure is necessary. The "short cut" method of settling such questions is never the best; though to those who read a chain of propositions without examining the separate links it may seem conclusive.

I remember to have seen an argument in favor of the proposition that "all men are now perfectly happy." It was constructed thus: "All men desire to be happy; there never was a man who wished to be miserable. The Creator is the author of this universal desire. He is omnipotent and beneficent, therefore he would not implant this desire without making it absolutely certain that it would be gratified; therefore all men always have been, and now are, perfectly happy." In the same way one might prove that all men are good. All desire to be happy. None but the good are happy, therefore all desire to be good; "but all that desire to be good are good, therefore all are good." The stern logic of experience contradicts these specious reasonings, and teaches us that we must ever be on our guard against "short cuts" to a conclusion. They may be sound, they may not be.

CHAPTER VI.

HOW THE THEATER IS DEFENDED—CONTINUED.

IT has been eloquently set forth by some that art is inferior only to religion in its elevating influence upon mankind; that the drama unites poetry, in its highest forms, with painting, and sculpture, and oratory, and music; and that to disparage it is vandalism, and springs from a spirit which would "destroy the sun because of its spots," and "hurl the world back on its path of progress." It is true that the drama blends all the arts in itself; that it is the product and illustration of them all; and that an abstract idea of a dramatic representation may be formed which would ennoble all who should behold it: but it is impossible to describe an existing institution by means of "glittering generalities." Painting, statuary, poetry, music, and oratory have all been made to promote licentiousness and irreligion as well as to assist religion. Because the spirit of poetry is allied to that of religion, it does not follow that *Queen Mab*, or the *Tragedy of Cain*, or *Don Juan* are of a religious tendency; or because Raphael's "Madonna," or Michael Angelo's "Judgment," are imbued with a devotional spirit, that all of the works of art unearthed at Pompeii are incentives to virtue. These generalities cannot be applied even to religion. Because religion is the friend and saviour of man it does not follow that there have not been religions which were worse than no religion at all; religions so corrupting as to imperil the very existence of society. When we praise religion we must know what religion we praise, and when we eulogize art we must distinguish its noble from its base uses. So that the whole question is open till we determine to what ends the music, and poetry, and oratory, and painting, of the Theater are made to contribute.

In defending the Theater it is said that it is a "school of morals;" that it "holds the mirror up to nature;" that virtue and its rewards, vice and its pains and penalties, are so skillfully, naturally, and truthfully represented, that good impressions are made; and that the evils are incidental and insignificant.

If we examine these statements we see at once that as the Theater deals with moral questions, it must be a "school of morals;" and as its methods of teaching are most impressive, it must be a very influential school. Hence, whether virtue and vice, with their results, are properly represented there, becomes a question of great importance. Nor would we be able to conclude our inquiries if it were found that virtue and vice are represented true to nature; for the vital point would still remain, whether it is beneficial to the moral nature to witness vice naturally delineated.

The foregoing are the principal views held of the stage by those of its friends who are not themselves actors; but there may be some who would indorse the estimate placed upon it by the actor Sothern, who, in a recent English paper, "aggrandizes his profession," at the same time expressing his opinion of the Church and the Press. He says: "The Drama is but an acted novel, and being acted, that is, presented in bodily form and audible speech, appeals even more vividly than mere written description to the masses, who have not the faculty of impersonating in their own minds the ideas of others, and to whom representation is essential. We wonder what the world would be without the Drama to 'hold, as 'twere, the mirror up to nature;' to show virtue her own features, scorn her own image, and 'the very age and body of the time its form and pressure;' had we no Othello, to warn us against jealousy; no School for Scandal, to ridicule that most fashionable vice; no Tartuffe, to gibbet hypocrisy; no Iago, to put us on our guard against our honest friends. In this material age and most matter-of-fact country, the Drama, either in its spoken or written form, is almost the sole intellectual element of our civilization; all else is Fact, sir; hard fact!... The Pulpit is so entirely given over to the exaltation of sect and dreams of the future life, to the utter neglect of all things pertaining to the present existence—deals so exclusively in *post-obits*—in fact, is so thoroughly polemical and retrogressive, that its power as a purifier and guide is almost naught. The press . . . is, by the necessity of the case, forced to neglect the lighter subjects, and so the Drama is left almost alone as a refining, elevating, and warning medium to that large majority of the world's inhabitants whose lack of time, opportunity, or taste for study prohibits any profound views to originate with themselves, and are, therefore, fain to accept the opinion of some 'guide, philosopher, and friend' to mold their crude views of things into shape and consistence." He further calls the Drama the "prop and mainstay of civilization," and would seem to have looked through one end of his telescope at the Drama, and through the other at the Church and the Press.

CHAPTER VII.

SENTIMENTS ADVERSE TO THE THEATER.

MANY of the opponents of the Theater declare that it is evil and only evil, and that continually; that no one can, under any circumstances, enter the Theater and be a Christian; and that even the desire to do so is ground for a strong presumption, if not a settled conviction, that the individual possessing such a desire is, if he professes to be a Christian, either a hypocrite or thoroughly self-deceived.

Every statement made in the interest of truth, which is inconsistent with facts defeats its own ends; and those who have for a time been imposed upon are rendered hostile to the truth itself when presented by those whom they have found unreliable. The charge that every play ever put on the boards is evil in matter and manner, cannot be maintained; that no dramatic representation has ever exerted a good influence is equally untenable;

that every actor is thoroughly immoral, is also incapable of proof; and, perhaps, in some instances a virtuous character has been as fully evinced by them as any thing of the nature can be; and to say that there have been no Christians, who have conscientiously supposed themselves at liberty to attend the Theater, is to say that there is no possibility of an error of judgment on this solitary question. Slavery. as an institution, was repugnant to Christian morality; but that good men erred in judgment thereupon will hardly be doubted. So there are different views of the true way to observe the Sabbath. Some hold an extremely rigid view, others are not so strenuous, and a respectable sect of Christians keep Saturday and work on Sunday. Shall we denounce those who differ in judgment from us as not worthy the name of Christians merely for that cause? So, even if it be believed that the Theater is "evil, and only evil, and that continually," let not him who, under that conviction, properly abhors the institution, abhor one who honestly holds a different opinion.

Others believe that there are fine sentiments in many plays; that but the smaller number are wholly evil; and that a mind thoroughly fortified by religion, observation, experience, and age, might attend certain dramatic representations without injury, and, perhaps, with pleasure and profit. But while they believe these things, they are compelled to believe, with equal confidence, that the character of plays in general is bad, and that the effect of the Theater upon its patrons is evil. They are also convinced that there are insuperable obstacles in the way of its reformation; and that Christians, in endeavoring to surmount them, would exhaust their energies to no good end. They think, furthermore, that in attempting to do so they would be obliged to turn aside from important fields of Christian effort which now call for greater fidelity than ever before, and that they would, by their example, lead many into temptations which they would not, perhaps could not, resist. And in addition to these evil results, and partly as a consequence of them, they think that the attendance of Christians on the Theater, and their attempt to elevate it, would lower the moral and religious tone of the Church, and diminish the influence of religion over the community in which the experiment should be tried. That it is the duty of all holding these views to remain away from the Theater and to dissuade others from attending, needs no argument. Whether the views of those who advocate, of those who apologize for, or of those who oppose, the Theater, are correct, every one must determine for himself after a careful examination.

CHAPTER VIII.

THE CHRISTIAN LIFE.

THUS far we have not inquired what it is to be a Christian, but certainly we must have a clear idea of this before we can determine whether a "Christian may with propriety do this or that." The term Christian is used to distinguish a man from Jews, Mohammedans, or Pagans. Again, the inhabitant of a Christian nation is, in a general sense, called a Christian. Coming a little nearer to the generic meaning of the word, a Christian is one who believes that Christ was an authoritative teacher of religion, philosophy, and morals. But still the meaning is too vague to signify much. The person may class him with Confucius or Buddha, and may himself be a Deist or a Pantheist.

To be a Christian is to endeavor to govern the life by the precepts of Christ, acknowledging him as an infallible authority in faith and morals, and relying upon him for salvation. For he said: "Ye are my friends, if ye do whatsoever I command you;" and again: "If ye love me keep my commandments." Or, as taught by an apostle: "Ye are not your own; for ye are bought with a price: therefore glorify God in your body, and in your spirit, which are God's," and, "Whether, therefore, ye eat, or drink, or whatsoever ye do, do all to the glory of God."

To be a Christian, therefore, is to decide on our conduct not by inclination, or selfish considerations, or the opinions of others, or the spirit of the time, or even by the example of the professedly pious, but by our settled and honest conviction of the will of Christ. But he has taught in his word that the heart must be filled with love to God and man; that the eye must be single if the whole body is full of light; that the body must be kept under subjection; that the principal aim of the life must be to love God and imitate Christ. Hence, a fundamental principle in determining the right or wrong of any proposed act is its relation to growth in the knowledge and love of God. If it promotes spiritual life, if it strengthens the soul to resist temptation, if it leads to clearer and more worthy conceptions of God and duty, if it increases love to Christians and to all men, and animates faith and hope, it is right. But if it is an impediment to piety and right living, if it diminishes the spirit of prayer or interest in spiritual things, if it disqualifies a person for earnest efforts to lead men to the consecration of their hearts and lives to God, it is wrong.

While these conclusions will not be questioned by any who are striving to be "dead unto the world, and alive unto Christ," it is nevertheless true that many things are allowable, right, and even necessary to the Christian whose tendency to assist him in a religious life is indirect, if at all discernible. The animal life must be maintained, hence the necessity for eating and drinking, for resting and sleeping. But these are acceptable unto God if we eat and drink for strength, and not for gluttony and drunkenness. Yet food eaten without relish is not promotive of health, hence it is right to prepare gratifications for the palate. Rest and sleep, also, are right, if they do not become the masters instead of the servants of the body; and though they may seem like a waste of time and strength, yet He who made us of the dust "knoweth our frame," with all its limitations, and so long as we do not sink into indolence and sloth, we may rest and sleep "to the glory of God."

But it has been found that something more than rest and sleep is necessary to preserve the body and mind in the best possible condition. Employment that is not *work*, a movement of body or mind which is spontaneous, causing and being accompanied by an unusual flow of spirits, is necessary, and such are its effects that it has been called recreation. A few persons whose labor is not exhausting, who are constantly traveling and mingling in society, or whose employment is of a most diversified character, may dispense with allotments of time for recreation, and a very few may pursue a monotonous business to old age, and despise amusement; but to most persons, especially in this high strung civilization, in which more of exhausting brain work is concentrated in a day than was demanded halt a century ago for the affairs of a week, it is essential for health, good spirits, and the best working condition, that some time should be devoted to relaxation, diversion, amusement, or whatever it may be called; and when it involves nothing immoral or pernicious, and is not carried so far as to become enervating, it can be done "to the glory of God."

Conversation, and music, and travel, and company, and healthful games, pictures, and calisthenics, and countless entertaining occupations, passive or active, here subserve a good purpose. And He who said unto his disciples "Come ye yourselves apart into a desert place, and rest awhile," can never condemn his tired servants if they loosen the bow which, if too long bent, will surely lose its elasticity. All will grant, however, that it would be improper to adopt as an amusement, without examination, any thing which may be suggested by others, or may occur to our own minds. It would not be maintained that he who professes to "live unto Christ" can seek amusement as the *end* of his life, any more than a man can be a Christian and make the sole object of his ambition the accumulation of wealth, or another live to eat instead of eating to live.

Nor should the Christian indulge in amusements

which are of such a character that he will be likely to be so fascinated by them as to interfere with the prosecution of the serious work of his life. It is also plain that any thing which appeals to the lower nature, the sensual appetites, must be discarded. These ever clamor for gratification, ever "obtrude beyond their proper sphere," and he who is taught by his Lord and Master to pray, "Lead us not into temptation," will not amuse himself by stimulating the source from which his most dangerous temptations and worst impulses arise. The rights of others must ever be regarded, and no known command of God violated. The spirit of cruelty, which in former ages pervaded the popular amusements of the world, is antagonistic to that of the Gospel. If a proposed amusement be injurious to the mind or body, it then defeats the only object for which it could with propriety be employed. But if its attractions are strong, but not dangerous—if it is healthful to the mind and body—if it does not excite the lower nature—if it does not inflict pain or disregard the rights or feelings of others—and if it be not carried so far as to occasion the neglect of duty or the expenditure of time without return or compensation which will justify it in the forum of conscience and reason—it is the privilege of the Christian, so far as it relates to his individual experience, to indulge in it. And from such amusement he may turn to work, or meditation, or prayer, with a conscience void of offense toward God or man on this account.

CHAPTER IX.

THE CHRISTIAN'S INFLUENCE.

IN the previous chapter we have spoken of the Christian's privilege as respects his individual experience. There is, however, a principle revealed in the Gospel, and powerfully urged, which may make it necessary for the Christian sometimes to deny himself an amusement which, to his own judgment, seems entirely unobjectionable. He may be obliged, in view of his relation to others, to say "all things are lawful for me, but all things are not expedient."

The duty of denying ourselves of voluntary gratifications when our indulgence in them would injure others, is a direct deduction from the Golden Rule. It finds its sublimest illustration in the sacrifice of Christ for us. The Apostle John (1 John iii, 16) deduces from that sacrifice the duty of the Christian to lay down his life, if necessary, for the brethren.

The logical clearness with which St. Paul states

this application of the law of love leaves nothing further to be said on the subject. As regards the opinion which we hold of what is right or wrong, "Let every man be fully persuaded in his own mind;" and we should not judge our brother, for he is not our servant, but Christ's, and "we shall all stand before the judgment-seat of Christ." "But if thy brother be grieved with thy meat, now walkest thou not charitably." "It is good neither to eat flesh, nor to drink wine, nor any thing whereby thy brother stumbleth, or is offended, or is made weak." "We then that are strong ought to bear the infirmities of the weak, and not to please ourselves. Let every one of us please his neighbor for his good to edification. For even Christ pleased not himself."

This duty of the Christian to deny himself for the benefit of his "weak brother" has never been very popular in the Church of Christ. Next to forgiving our enemies, and praying for them that despitefully use us, it is the most difficult task imposed upon the average Christian. It has been said that "this weak brother is the greatest bully in the universe," that he attempts to abridge our liberty in Christ Jesus, to place us under a yoke of bondage, and that yoke made of his narrow prejudices. To the "weak brother" who proposes to *domineer* over us there is but one answer: "Who art thou that judgest another man's servant? to his own master he standeth or falleth; yea, he shall be holden up: for God is able to make him stand." "All things are lawful for me." But it is not the case of the bullying "weak brother" that is contemplated in these inspired directions. "Him that is weak in the faith receive ye, but not to doubtful *disputations*." Receive the "weak brother," but not to give him authority over your faith. If he "bullies," the Christian must assert his liberty in Christ Jesus, and the other must learn humility.

But the case provided for is this: When the Christian sees that for him to do a certain thing, the doing or not doing being voluntary, will put a stumbling-block in his brother's way, or grieve him, or make him weak, he being conscious of his own strength, holding his faith and freedom before God, must "bear the infirmities of the weak, and not please" himself, rather must he "please his neighbor for his good to edification." This voluntary surrender under the law of love, and in the "imitation of Christ," for the sake of "the weak brother," is a very different thing from being "bullied" by him into a cowardly and unwilling relinquishment of our rights.

But, strangely or otherwise, most believers are more favorably impressed with the declaration, "All things are lawful for me," than with that which follows, "All things are not expedient;" and again, "All things edify not." Is this because the assertion of freedom is more congenial to human nature than the recognition of the duty of restraint on account of, as it often seems to us, the contemptible and inexcusable prejudices of others?

The application through love of others of this self-denial to amusements is just what it is to other questions. We may not amuse ourselves in such a way that our example will lead others into dangerous positions. He would not be thought a kind or discreet parent who, in the presence of children, would amuse himself with fire-arms and then leave them loaded where those children could reach them. Nor is he who indulges, in promiscuous society, in the use of intoxicating liquors, even though he honestly claims a right to use them for himself, acting charitably toward those who will by his act "look upon the wine when it is red," even though "at the last it biteth like a serpent, and stingeth like an adder." He, therefore, who would "please his neighbor for his good to edification," will indulge in no amusement whose general effect is bad, even though upon himself it may be indifferent, or even, as he supposes, good.

Again, it is the duty of the Christian to "walk in wisdom toward them that are without," and this wisdom has respect to the word of Christ: "As thou hast sent me into the world, even so have I sent them into the world," that men might "believe in me through their word." Whence it follows that no faithful disciple of Christ can amuse himself by what he believes will weaken his influence as a Christian. But it may be asked, Is there no limitation to the application of this principle? What subject is there on which none have prejudices?

The inquiry is both pertinent and difficult. The wearing of beards by the ministry has offended many, and the mustache in the pulpit yet disturbs some; the introduction of instrumental music into churches, the disuse of the white cravat, countless things used and disused, have grieved many.

In the matter of amusement some believe that none is necessary, while others admit its rightfulness, and yet condemn in detail every possible form. A recent but very popular game, as much used by clergymen and Christians as among irreligious people, is denounced by some as "billiards in disguise," and as "Satan's principal card in the game which he is playing with the Church." I admit that there is a limit, and of that limit the Christian must seriously judge for himself, and ask in every instance, "Is this one of the things which I ought to avoid for the sake of my brethren, and that my influence as a Christian may not be diminished? or is it of such a nature that I may indulge in it, trusting to my general character and influence to counteract any incidental evils?"

In all cases where there is not an express command, we must at the last retreat to our own best judgment. But the word of God is explicit in teaching that we cannot decide merely that an act is *lawful*, and then proceed to perform it, *regardless of its effect upon our brethren*, and *our influence over the irreligious.* We must also decide whether it, though proper, as we conceive, in itself, will have such an influence that we should deny ourselves of it for the sake of others; and if we decide that it will, we are to give it up joyfully for "his sake" and for "conscience' sake;" "conscience, I say, not thine own, but *of the other:* for why is my liberty judged of another man's conscience?"

CHAPTER X.

The Impulses and Tastes of Youth.

THE Theater always has been and must be chiefly attended and supported by the young. And investigation shows that in every audience as many as two thirds are under thirty years of age. This would be so if the Theater attracted all classes of the population equally, for but little more than one third are over thirty years old. But as age advances the love of amusement, as such, in many persons diminishes, and the loss of novelty, the increase of cares, the demands on money, and the decline of health, all tend to reduce the attendance on expensive and late evening entertainments of every kind. And as very young children are seldom taken, we are, probably, much below the truth in stating that as many as two thirds of the persons composing every ordinary assembly in the Theater are between the ages of fifteen and thirty.

In determining, therefore, whether the Theater, as

an institution, should receive the support of Christians, we must keep the fact that it chiefly influences youth and young men and women clearly before our minds. Now there are principles concerning the impulses and tastes of youth, as well as the peculiar dangers to which they are exposed, that are as certain as any thing which experience and observation teach, and these must be applied in estimating the probable influence of the Theater. Among these principles the following are most important, and bear directly on the solution of the problem. Liberty and license are peculiarly charming to the young, and especially to young men; while the idea of restraint is entirely distasteful to them, and those who impose it are disliked in proportion to the extent of their power and persistency.

Quiet living and self-denial are attained by painful discipline. Many and bitter are the lessons which the high-spirited youth must learn before he can be brought to adopt, as the rule of his life, a willing and rational denial to himself of present gratification for future good. And often the very qualities which would make the young man, if he practice self-denial, pre-eminently powerful and useful, will ruin him most speedily and hopelessly if he does not deny himself.

Equally true is it that a horror of vice, arising from a conviction and vivid apprehension of its sinfulness and of its dreadful consequences, is the best safeguard for youth. Familiarity with vice in any form, before the mind and conscience are thoroughly fortified against temptation, and habits of right living are established, is dangerous in the extreme.

It is also known and admitted by all thoughtful observers, that the gratification of irregular impulses in youth forms a habit sooner than similar gratifications in adult years. The nature is more plastic and there is less power of self-control. Besides, the blood then courses more wildly through the veins, and excitement yields more pleasure. Lord Byron had this in view when he wrote:—

"Ah, vice, how soft are thy voluptuous ways!
When boyish blood is mantling, who can 'scape,
The fascination of thy magic gaze?
A cherub hydra round us thou dost gape,
And mold to every taste thy dear delusive shape."

And what is as pertinent, and in its consequences as baneful, is, that when such a habit is formed in youth it is much more difficult to shake it off than when it was not begun till middle life.

The system has, in the former case, "grown to the act," and a positive change has taken place in the structure; while in the latter all the preceding tendencies are against the permanent domination of a new course of action. Hence we know that it is comparatively rare that bad habits, whose foundation was not laid in the excesses of youth, are formed after middle life, excepting in the cases where morals, in extreme age, deteriorate with the accession of dotage, an occurrence more frequent than those who never gave the subject any attention may suppose. And we also know that when the evil habits set up in youth are persisted in through early manhood, the probabilities of their ever being shaken off greatly and rapidly diminish with every succeeding year; and that to break them up at any stage after they have been fairly entered upon, is like "wrenching a bone from its socket."

Another fact of great significance is, that morbid habits are much more persistent than those which fall in with the healthful operations of nature or the legitimate obligations of life. It is more difficult to give up the use of opium, alcohol, or even tobacco, than to deny one's self any one kind of wholesome food; and it is much harder to prevent the rising of lascivious thoughts, when allowed long or frequently to absorb the attention, than to destroy any habit of reflection or occupation which does not awaken or stimulate the passions. Such abnormal habits become "second nature," and often enchain the victim in a thraldom more abject and pitiless than the first nature, even where that is intensified by a strong hereditary predisposition, would ordinarily maintain over any responsible being.

CHAPTER XI.

PRINCIPLES INVOLVED IN THEATRICAL REPRESENTATIONS.

THE success of a theatrical entertainment depends largely upon its power to fasten the attention and excite the emotions. And representation and costume, the voice and the living person, make a much deeper impression, and produce in most minds, if not all, a more intense excitement, than reading or study, however protracted or profound. The introduction of different characters, the whole scenery resembling real life, produces an illusion in susceptible minds which has been properly expressed by the word "entranced." And this effect, if the sentiments advanced be elevating, is good, and if they be immoral, it is bad. But it is a point of great weight and positive bearing whether the virtues are capable of yielding such intense excitement as the vices.

It will, I think, be conceded either at once, or

after a little reflection, that truth, honesty, temperance, industry, frugality, chastity, and, in general, religion, are not capable of being represented in the Theater, either in matter or manner, so as to cause such intense excitement as vice and its entanglements, as intrigue, drunkenness, duelling, conspiracy, adultery, divorce, treason, robbery, forgery, the altering of wills, murder, incest, and the passions which occasion these crimes, namely, lust, revenge, covetousness, and ambition. The virtues which in actual life are quiet and unobtrusive, could be worked up to excite only by bringing the vices into proximity to them, and delineating so vividly the temptation as to make it long doubtful how the scale would turn; and then if it should always turn on the side of virtue it would often be against the sympathies of many, and in a brief period become monotonous to most. Thus the two grand divisions of the Drama, tragedy and comedy, deal chiefly with sins and vices, either alone, or in terrible and long uncertain conflict with virtue. The very idea of tragedy involves a fatal issue, or a fatal issue unexpectedly escaped; while that of comedy includes foibles, sins which are comical in their effects, and in general the ludicrous accidents of life.

There is, however, a limit to the interest which the Christian can take in the representation of scenes of vice. It cannot be proper to hear or see voluntarily, for the sake of pleasure, what it would be improper to say or do. If the doing of sinful things is sinful, "to have pleasure in them that do them" must be sinful also, for the same state of mind is implied in both cases. If there are in plays profane expressions, or indecent allusions, or lascivious looks, attitudes, and gestures, it cannot be right to derive amusement from the spectacle.

We speak now, not of the crimes represented, but of the language and attitudes employed in representing them. Hence, the Christian could find no pleasure in much that would create great interest in an assembly of average morality; and what is considered by a sagacious "management actually necessary to success," would be regarded as sinful by any one who adopts the precepts of Christ as the rule of his life.

CHAPTER XII.

GENERAL CHARACTERISTICS OF PLAYS — THE MATTER.

BELIEVING the principles set forth in the preceding chapters to be evident, we will now make a discriminating examination of the Theater in this country with respect chiefly to the fundamental elements of matter and manner. And there are certain general characteristics of plays which will be at once recognized, and hardly denied by any.

Christian principles are not accepted as the rule of morals. Praise and censure are not given according to the precepts of the Gospel, but according to shifting, worldly, and often immoral, codes. Hence, the Theater cannot teach the morals of Christianity to those whom it influences; but, so far as it departs therefrom, it diminishes the hold which Christian morality has upon the public. That which Christianity denounces as a great sin is often spoken of as a mere folly or insignificant defect of character. And a mode of life which Christ enjoins on his disciples is disparaged as superfluous or impossible.

True religion—meaning the conscientious, self-denying, world-renouncing, God-fearing, Christian—is never praised, but usually ridiculed; and when religion comes upon the stage it is generally in the person of a sporting parson, or an *Aminadab Sleek*, or the *Hypocrite*. If an instance of whole-souled benevolence is brought forward, it is usually an act performed by some "good liver," some "hale fellow;" and if a piece of penuriousness is to be denounced, not unfrequently it is connected with some "sanctimonious" professor. That religion of an easy-going sort is sometimes complimented, is freely admitted; and that many fine and just sentiments concerning God, and virtue, and the future life are introduced, is well known. But that the kind of piety that denies self, renounces the world, and fears God, is seldom or never praised in the literature of the Drama, will be denied by none who are familiar with the subject.

A few plays have been written in which conscientious piety has been justly commended and illustrated, but they never became popular, and it is difficult to name one that was ever performed three times in the same place. And yet this is the only kind of piety to which the promise of salvation is annexed—a piety which is distasteful to man until he is renewed by the Holy Spirit, and which even then requires much prayer and self-denial to bear its burdens and discharge its duties.

Again, in most plays, wickedness is made to furnish amusement. Lying, drunkenness, adultery, and "other" works of the flesh, "become the cause of sport," and the occasion of hilarity. And, as it has been truly said, "Crimes that would call down the wrath of God on their perpetrators are systematically made to provoke laughter."

To this charge it may be said, "Such is life; the newspapers abound with accounts of similar crimes daily committed among us; history is full of them." This, alas! is too true; but who, if his moral sense be acute, would read them anywhere, or behold them for diversion, or otherwise than from necessity, and with feelings of real horror. On the stage one character is introduced "who incessantly lies;" another, who steals; another, who is always drinking and reveling; another, who is conspiring; another, who attempts intrigue; another, who poisons; another, who commits adultery or murder: and though some of these actions are not now, as they were at one time, actually represented before the spectators, yet all is done to produce the illusion that they are really happening. Oaths and profane expressions are often introduced, and in some popular plays are used by the actors more frequently than they occur in the original text. Witticisms, whose whole point lies in an indecent allusion or implication, are very common; and in many cases if the open obscenity, the licentious wit, the profaneness, and the turns of expression which run along the confines of impropriety, always apparently about to cross, but just escaping, were expurgated, there would be little left to excite, or even to hold, attention.

Much is sometimes said of the "moral" of the play being good. As a rule, where there is any moral, in the technical sense of that word, it is hastily disposed of in the fifth act. But this cannot counteract the evil influence of what has preceded it.

Suppose a story for youth, full of reckless adventures, illicit loves, profane and vulgar witticisms, in which the characters have a good time, and though getting into many perplexities generally extricate themselves by their own ingenuity, or escape by some stroke of fortune, is it to be believed, or even fancied, that if on the last page it should be stated that the "way to be happy is to be good," or the "path of duty is the path of safety," the effect of the previous narrative would be favorably modified?

It is sometimes affirmed that this objection, that plays contain obscene allusions, would condemn the Bible. This reply will have force when *one* passage can be found in the Bible in which a word was introduced for the *sake* of its obscenity. And the attempt to bolster up the filthy allusions in plays by the Bible will be seen to be as absurd as it is profane when we remember, that from the sixty-six different books of which the Bible is composed, not an instance can be produced of a joke founded on licentiousness or sin, while its solemn declaration is, that neither "drunkards," nor "thieves," nor "fornicators," nor "adulterers," nor "liars," nor "profane" swearers, nor "murderers," "shall inherit the kingdom of God."

CHAPTER XIII.

HOW PLAYS ARE PUT UPON THE STAGE.

THUS far we have spoken of the matter of plays; but when we inquire into the manner in which they are put upon the stage it becomes apparent that good impressions cannot be made. To sit unmoved, coldly critical, saying to one's self, "This is but fiction," would not admit of much enjoyment. The greater the sympathetic excitement the more exquisite the emotion. The spectator must laugh with him that laughs, rave with him that raves, and weep with him that weeps; or if the play be such as to require sympathy with one character and antipathy to another, this feeling must be maintained all the way through.

The terror-stricken old lady who, being at the Theater for the first time, cried out, "Are you going to let him kill her right here!" as a disappointed lover was about to plunge his dagger into the heart of a young woman, was in the state to get the greatest enjoyment could she but have suppressed the absurd outcry. Lord Byron had a convulsion under Kean's acting of "Sir Giles Overreach;" many ladies went into hysterics; and even a "veteran actress was so overpowered by the last speech of Sir Giles that she absolutely fainted on the stage." If the sentiment of the play were unexceptionable the highest moral results could not be produced under such conditions; but if the play be immoral, none but the worst effects can follow.

If it be thought that the same objection might be urged against oratory and the excitement which it produces, it is necessary only to suggest that whenever oratory is so employed as to dethrone the judgment, and govern the hearer wholly by his impulses, it is objectionable in the highest degree; and when it is employed to persuade men to vice or irreligion, or unjustifiable treason, or to give an unrighteous verdict, it is a curse and not a blessing. But when oratory produces the feelings which reason and morals approve, it may intensify them with benefit to any degree not incompatible with a rational self-control.

The objection against the excitement of the Theater is, that it is the greatest possible to be caused by the surrender of the judgment to the illusion, and that the matter received is not such as to improve the character, but to loosen the springs of virtue and purity; and that the sympathies are very often, if not generally, drawn out by and to improper objects.

It is a consideration which, if duly weighed, will be seen to possess great force, that the appearance, dress, expression, language, and attitude of actors must, and do correspond, as far as possible, to the characters assumed. The woman of easy virtue, the young woman being led astray, the libertine, the gambler, the reveler, the traducer—all these must dress and act in character. The law of God declares that the indulgence of the sexual passions out of wedlock is a sin of the deepest malignity. The imagination on this subject is the ally and procuress of the passions, and without exception the most terrible moral strain imposed on youth is to be pure in thought, feeling, and act. These things being so, is it possible that the spectacle of women, painted, dressed as they are, with heaving bosoms, languishing glances, voluptuous attitudes, falling into the arms of men with whom they are on the verge, according to the play, of committing adultery, should make any other than the worst possible impressions? Persons of mature years and thorough self-mastery have found such spectacles to "tempt them to immorality;" while to expect the young to behold them without their imaginations being polluted is to defy reason and experience.

But we are compelled by the truth to probe this subject still further, and to maintain that the excitement of the sympathies upon fictitious objects is enervating and pernicious. When the sympathies are awakened by the spectacle of real distress, there is a strong inward prompting to relieve the sufferer. It is well known that if that inward prompting be repressed, after a time suffering will not awaken the emotion. But when the sympathies are excited on fictitious objects, and there is no need or opportunity of relief, it comes to pass that the sympathies only are excited by real suffering, and the prompting to relieve is no longer felt. This explains the paradoxical spectacle too often seen of eyes streaming with tears of sympathy, and hands making no effort, or but a feeble one, to relieve.

Another law of human nature affects the heart perniciously. It is necessary that every thing should be accomplished in an evening. A man is married, bereaved or divorced, married again, his children grow, estates are divided, all kinds of complications, fearful disasters, such as would naturally be diffused through many years, crowd upon the spectator in rapid succession; and if he give himself up to the effect he becomes drunk with passion—whether pity, sympathy, love, fear, joy, or hate. When such a man or woman returns to real life ordinary distress fails to move him, and they who weep over imaginary scenes leave suffering work people unpaid, and consider it annoying to be solicited for charitable objects.

The liberality of some actors is sometimes adduced to show the contrary of what is here asserted. But the charity of actors is usually lavish generosity; a profusion fully in harmony with their general character and way of living. Most of them, by their own confession regardless of pecuniary obligation, will either spend or give their money according to their changing impulses. How little does this, like the reckless gifts of a Fisk or the politic benefactions of a Tweed, resemble the regular, self-denying, and conscientious efforts of a liberal and well-balanced mind to diminish the griefs or promote the welfare of his fellow-men!

It is true that performances are often given for the benefit of certain popular charities, for the relief of poverty-stricken actors, and the widows and orphans of firemen, etc. Just so far as such appropriations are made from motives of charity they deserve approbation, and the writer has no desire to withhold it; but where the advantages of an extensive advertisement, and the expectation that many Christians will relax their ordinary strictness "for the sake of the cause," and that having once obtained a "taste of the nectar, they will continue to drink it," are the controlling motives, the appropriation deserves no more commendation than that which is to be given to not very scrupulous shrewdness.

CHAPTER XIV.

GROUNDS ON WHICH THESE STATEMENTS ARE MADE.

IT is often said that those who oppose the Theater do so under the influence of unreasoning prejudice. When asked if they have ever attended a theatrical exhibition they admit that they have not, and are then told that they "do not know what they are talking about," and that if "they were to visit the Theater they would change their sentiments concerning the propriety of attending it."

It would by no means follow, that enough cannot be ascertained of the tendency of an institution, or a particular line of conduct, without personal experience to determine whether it is good or evil. May not the evils of gambling be ascertained without visiting gambling saloons, and its fascination be proved as a fact by one who has never gambled? Is it necessary to become a drunkard, or to frequent bar-rooms and groggeries, to obtain satisfactory reasons for adopting temperance principles! If we study the changes that take place in men's conduct and characters we can determine the nature of the influences to which they have been exposed. And by this method it would be sufficiently easy to show that the elements of the charges made against the matter and manner of the Theater are not imaginary but real. But we have the advertisements, and programmes, and *critiques* in the great daily papers, and from these we may deduce abundant evidence that the Theater ought not to be attended or supported by Christians. If it be what it *promises* to be—what the critics affirm *that it is*—its general character is not such that the Christian can find innocent pleasure in visiting it.

The writer, in his youth, was for a brief period fascinated by the Theater. The time, indeed, was short, but the fever raged. During his attendance thereon, amounting to perhaps thirty visits, he saw some of the most noted actors who have appeared in this country during the last quarter of a century—some of whom are still in the front rank of their profession. The influence of this course upon his moral and religious character was decidedly bad. The sneers at religion and "strait-laced bigots," which certain comedies contained, embittered him toward a life of piety. The excitement of the evening unfitted him for the serious pursuit of his business. He lost relish for lectures and solid reading; his manner, even, underwent a change, and now a semi-tragical extravagance and then an infusion of comical slang came into his mode of speaking and acting. It seemed "smart" to him then, but in the retrospect it appears contemptible. Besides, the company into which he was thrown was generally of a character injurious to the morals of a young man, and as he gained a relish for it he lost all interest in that of steady persons. And he firmly believes that if, by a determined effort, under the influence of an aroused conscience awakened by the contrast between the recklessness of life toward which he was tending and that course of piety which had been inculcated upon him by the precept and example of his parents, he had not broken away from his companions and given up Theaters and kindred forms of dissipation, he would have been ruined.

In urging, therefore, the young to abstain from the Theater, and holding that it is wrong for the Christian to countenance it, we "do know what we are talking about," so far as experience can impart that knowledge. Nor are our conclusions drawn from an exceptional case. The writer was neither better nor worse than his companions. And possessing a lively recollection of the influence exerted over himself, he has narrowly observed the unfolding of character among the large numbers of youth with whom he has been thrown, and has conversed with many who have had opportunities similar to his own. And from the whole he can draw but two conclusions, namely:—

That there is no habit, which does not imply a positive renunciation of morality, more pernicious than that of Theater-going; and that whatever may have occurred in isolated cases, he who intends to live a thoroughly religious life must renounce the Theater. And if, after having made the attempt, he returns to his former habits, a great change for the worse in his moral and spiritual condition will soon be seen.

CHAPTER XV.

PLAYS PRESENTED IN NEW YORK DURING THE PAST THREE YEARS.

BEING aware of the fact that the Drama, like every thing else which caters to the taste, has its fashions—rising and falling and undergoing various changes—now improving and then degenerating, I have thought it desirable to institute a careful inquiry into the plays which have been performed in the principal theaters of New York during the past three years.

Accordingly I procured the copies used by the performers in preparing for their parts, and took pains to ascertain wherein, in actual use, the actors diverged from the printed copy. They number over sixty, and, with the exception of a few unpublished plays, include all that have been produced in the prominent Theaters of New York during the three years now about closing. And the inquiry has been carried on upon no narrow determination to find in every play proof of a preconceived theory. Sentiments and forms of expression which many, whose taste has been formed under the influence of a severely religious life, would throw out as faults, have often been considered by the writer as blemishes, and the judgment of those who differ with him on the general subject called in to decide in particular cases.

Nor has much attention been given to the lower order of Theaters, where the principal and avowed aim is to please the most coarse and depraved tastes; but most of the plays examined have been produced in the Theaters patronized by the highest circles of society.

The results of this examination confirm the charges which we have made. Some of the plays produced are in matter unobjectionable, but the number of such is very small in proportion to the whole. Some instances occurred in which, where the original composition was unexceptionable, the attempt was made, by dress, attitude, emphasis, and look, to please that large part of every audience that cannot be entranced by a chaste performance.

These attempts have from time to time been rebuked by the critics of the higher tone, not so much, indeed, on the ground of their immorality, as because of their violation of artistic propriety.

It is a singular fact, that, with three or four exceptions, those dramatic compositions among the sixty or more under discussion, which are morally unobjectionable, are of a comparatively low order of literary execution. But if language and sentiments which would not be tolerated among respectable people, and would excite indignation if addressed to the most uncultivated and coarse servant girl, not openly vicious, by an ordinary young man, and profaneness which would brand him who uttered it as irreligious are improper amusements for the young and for Christians of every age, then at least fifty of these plays are to be condemned.

Not all are as bad as the worst, but many are so corrupting that one of the chief illustrations of their evil tendency, and of the demoralizing influence of the Theater is, that such a number can be found to defend them. *She Stoops to Conquer*, Goldsmith's well known and popular play, is based on a rake's going to a country house to woo the owner's daughter, mistaking the mansion for an inn, and attempting to persuade the daughter, who is taken for a barmaid, to licentiousness. The hero exhibits some noble traits, one of which is, that while he thought nothing of adultery or fornication, he would shrink from seducing an innocent girl. The play contains much profaneness and vulgarity, and several sneers at temperance and religion.

There are persons who will look with lofty scorn on the above characterization of *She Stoops to Conquer.* They will say that the stern moralist, Dr. Johnson, told his friend, Bishop White, that he thought it worthy of a "very kind reception." This, indeed, will not seem wonderful when the personal relations between Johnson and Goldsmith are remembered. But the whole teaching of Samuel Johnson, on which his reputation as a moralist is founded, condemns the play which his personal regard for the author led him to commend.

It is said that Goldsmith questioned one of his critics thus: "Did it make you laugh?" "Exceedingly," replied the critic. "Then," said the author, "that is all I require." The play is certainly admirably adapted to provoke laughter; but we propound this question: Are lust and attempted libertinism, profaneness, falsehood, and intemperance the things at which *Christians should laugh?* If we traduce the play we deserve reproof; but if we describe it correctly, the scorn of those who approve it is natural enough on their part, and simply confirmatory of our position.

Money is a succession of hypocrisy, covetousness, drinking, gambling, jealousy, and infidelity, adapted to impart a view of life to the young, which, if taken as true, would lead to distrust, misanthropy, and personal recklessness. *East Lynn* consists of infidelity, adultery, murder, remarriage, and the subsequent reappearance of the first wife to die in the house of her former husband.

CHAPTER XVI.

PLAYS PRESENTED IN NEW YORK DURING THE PAST THREE YEARS—CONTINUED.

THE atmosphere of the *Ticket-of-Leave Man* is similar to that of "pirate and murder books," and its style such as to familiarize the mind with scenes of vice and desperate wickedness, and the ear with coarseness and slang. This play is said to have reformed one or more highwaymen and desperadoes. It may have done so; but if so, it was upon the principle that some medicines which would poison a well man will, in certain abnormal states of the system, work a favorable change.

Saratoga is to be condemned for its profaneness and its "*double entente*," but much more for the spirit of falsehood and perfidy which pervades it. The effect of the characters, attitudes, and sentiments of the piece cannot be good. It is one of those productions which diminish respect for woman, and dissipate all serious views of life. No doubt some parts of it are tolerably correct descriptions of the life of insincerity and folly to which many devote themselves at Saratoga and elsewhere, but the general tendency is to familiarize the mind with impure thoughts, improper words, unchaste feelings, and immoral conduct. Nor is there a sentiment in it which disparages the life which it describes, unless it be the profane growling of Remington *pere* or the moralizing of the nurse. To read it would be detrimental to youth for the same reason that certain inferior kinds of fiction would injure them, and to see it would affect them for evil just as would an evening in bad company. And though in this case, as in the others, many may be found to say "it never did me any harm," may it not be either that "no harm" is done them, because they are already down to its level and saturated with its spirit; or are not proper judges of whether they are harmed or not. The elements of which a thing is composed determine its tendency; and so long as it is true that "evil communications corrupt good manners" so long will such a play as *Saratoga* be indefensible as a legitimate amusement.

The *School for Scandal* is a play the whole of which no woman could read to any but her husband, or some other near relative, without giving ground for a presumption against her purity; and there are in it many sentences and witty turns which no gentleman could use even among gentlemen without incurring the charge of lewdness in his talk. As recently remodeled for one of the principal theaters in New York, the editor feels constrained to apologize for its moral tendencies. In this apology the convenient method, so often employed in defending a bad case, is resorted to, and he omits to attempt the defense of the worst parts, and calls an assignation and the attempted debauching of a married woman, the success of which was prevented by an accident, a "peccadillo"—indeed, he can hardly call it that, but speaks of it as a "supposed peccadillo."

As a specimen of the moral sense developed by the Theater, we give a paragraph of the editor's apology for the *School for Scandal:* "Fault has often been found with the moral tendencies of the piece; and it must be confessed that the spendthrift injustice of Charles is too leniently dealt with.

We could never admire that species of generosity which would rob a creditor to lavish money upon one who might have been in no greater want of it than he to whom it was legally due. *Sir Peter Teazle* is the least objectionable character in the piece, morally considered; and even *he* is disposed to make light of the *supposed* peccadillo of Joseph in the fourth act, until he finds that the lady behind the screen is his own wife."

But the play has more than a score of filthy allusions in it, and deals with adultery and fornication in the loosest way. Nor can the oft-quoted reply, "evil to him who evil thinks," be used with propriety against our criticism: for that is applicable only when a sentence is capable of two interpretations, one pure the other impure, and there is no reason to suppose that the impure is the *sense intended* by the author. In such a case he who insists on the impure interpretation deserves the rebuke; but the allusions in the *School for Scandal* are capable *of but one* interpretation, and are undeniably introduced for their impurity. And yet a short time since, in a literary society, a lady belonging to an excellent family spoke in an essay in the most glowing terms of this piece, for which even the actors themselves have been compelled to apologize! This "color blindness" is the fruit of familiarity with such compositions.

And what ought we to say of a *New Way to Pay Old Debts?* It must be freely admitted that it contains some fine sentiments and magnificent turns of expression, among the finest of which is this: "And Heaven here gives a precedent to teach us, that when men leave religion and turn atheists their own abilities leave them." Another is this: "You dare do any ill; yet want true valor to be honest, and repent." But there is a fatal defect in the moral teaching of the play, which will be obvious to every one who has read it, or to whom it may be pointed out. The principal character is punished for his infamous plots and villainies, not by the providence of God, not by civil law, not by the honest work of honest men; but he is overcome by counterplots, and betrayed by one of his own minions, to whom, after he has used him, the man who marries the heroine addresses these words:— "You are a rascal; and he that dares be false to a master, *though unjust*, will very hardly be true to any other."

I admit that very often the wicked are thus overthrown, and that so far the piece is true to nature; but the effect of the play is rather to create the impression that in contending with a villain all means are lawful; that if he is a plotter or swindler, he may be overcome by similar modes. That this criticism *is just*, and not strained, appears from the fact that it has been found necessary to attempt to vindicate the play from the charge, and in the attempt the method of defense fully supports the charge.

In the editorial introduction to my copy the following passage occurs: "It has been objected to this play that Margaret, who is otherwise recommended to our sympathies by the most charming feminine traits, should be concerned in the plot for deceiving her father; but the author questioned nature on this point, and her answer decided him in his course. How improbable that the daughter of a man so reckless and unyielding as Sir Giles would have been withheld by any squeamish considerations of the obligations of filial candor and duty, where her affections for her lover were likely to be thwarted! We do not vindicate her disingenuousness; but we doubt if the best men would not at the crisis feel themselves authorized to use the devil's weapons in outwitting the devil. A simple-minded girl, shrinking beneath the insupportable violence of such a tyrant, resorts as naturally to craft for her escape as the ground bird does, who would mislead the trampling school-boy as to the position of her nest."

We do not doubt the statement that most men would use the "devil's weapons to outwit the devil;" but when the "devil's weapons" are used, it is generally the devil who conquers, for those weapons are edged in every part, and cut the hand that smites as well as the foe that is smitten.

One of the charges we made against plays in general is, that they do not teach Christian morals, but fall in with the instincts and passions of man; and this defense of Margaret's duplicity is a bold avowal of the propriety of "doing evil that good may come," a doctrine which, generally believed and practiced, would undermine the whole fabric of morals and religion, whose root principle is, "Be not overcome of evil, but overcome evil with good."

Led Astray is a well-known comedy which had a long run, and will continue to be popular. The writer has heard two persons whom he respects, one an elderly lady the other an intelligent young gentleman, praise this piece as wholly unobjectionable in a moral point of view. Said both in substance, There is not a sentiment or situation in it to which the most fastidious could object.

Having procured a copy the writer read it, and was surprised at what his friends had said. It is not very profane, nor are there many obscene remarks in it. But in less than half the first act there are many allusions to amorous intrigues; and as the play progresses indecent situations increase, while the whole of the plot runs along the verge of a double adultery —that of the unappreciative husband and the sentimental wife. The presumption is, that the former fell; the latter seems to have wandered in spirit, and burned incense in her heart to an idol for many months, but through the intervention of a watchful cousin escaped plunging into the vortex.

The writer invited one of the persons who had praised the moral tendency, the language, and the situations of the comedy to reread it with him. On being asked whether he heard "this," and "this," he recollected the greater part, but some of the most objectionable features were unnoticed or had escaped his recollection; but there they were, and the writer had ascertained that they were produced. What is the explanation of the "obliquity of vision" that defends the indefensible? In some cases, it is that familiarity with such representations obscures the perceptions; and in others, that the mind is so absorbed in the progress of events that all power of discrimination is lost, and the most objectionable ideas, feelings, and phrases are imperceptibly imbibed, and, it is to be feared, assimilated.

CHAPTER XVII.

PLAYS PRESENTED IN NEW YORK DURING THE PAST THREE YEARS—CONTINUED.

WE will now speak of *London Assurance*, a comedy whose popularity has been sustained for more than thirty years: but notwithstanding this fact we maintain that it should receive no countenance from the Christian, or from persons whose moral principles are in harmony with the New Testament, or from those who desire the elevation of social life. It is published as No. 27 of French's Standard Dramas, edited by Epes Sargent, whose introduction thus abundantly supports the ground we take:—

"A notable defect in the play is the heartlessness and flippancy of its pervading tone. *Max Harkaway*, who is a mere repetition of the fox-hunting country gentleman of innumerable comedies, is the only individual of the *dramatis personæ*, who seems to have the most distànt notion of a moral obligation or a generous impulse. It is not the absence of 'noble sentiments,' but of redeeming traits, to which we allude. The *Courtlys*, father and son, are weak, unprincipled libertines, the fool prevailing in one and the scamp in the other. *Lady Gay Spanker* is a monstrous, and, we trust, a wholly imaginary creation. No woman of any pretensions to breeding or good sense would treat a husband, were he ever so much of an ass, in the manner she does. It is a libel upon decent society to suppose that it could tolerate such a creature. *Grace Harkaway*, from the fustian put into her mouth, is apparently intended for a romantic simpleton. The author has certainly succeeded in making her a very uninteresting one. *Meddle*, the lawyer, though a broad caricature, is a very laughable one; and as members of his profession afford popular subjects for ridicule and abasement, the introduction of this part may have contributed materially to the favorable reception of the piece. In all these pretended portraitures of some of the constituents of respectable English society, we look in vain for any thing like earnestness of character. Not an indication does any one give that he is conscious of the possession of a soul. All appear to be playing a part—striving to *seem*, rather than to *be*. Emotion is voted vulgar, and a show of sincerity is evidently regarded as precluding the claims of the comedy to the title of fashionable. . . . But in the present play the darker sides of human character are exclusively presented; and on rising from the representation, we always feel, in spite of the elegant saloons and gilded furniture, that we have been in indifferently honest company. The climax of absurdity is reached when the moralizing speech at the close, on the qualities of a gentleman, is put into the lips of the old miscreant who has just been disappointed in his design of running away with another man's wife."

The preceding criticism, let it be remembered, was not written by a "Pharisee," or a "Quaker," or a "bigot," or even by "a ranting preacher," but by a Dramatic Editor, for the use of actors, and bears the imprint of the most celebrated dramatic publishing house. Judged, however, by Christian morality, severer charges even than these might be maintained against it.

The Belle's Stratagem, though written by Mrs. Hannah Cowley, a woman of unquestioned ability, is a most licentious production, full of attempted intrigue, and abounding in base deceptions. No sophistry can gloss it over; and the introduction here and there of fine sentiments, can no more justify the play as a whole than occasional acts of courtesy and refined expressions can make a boor a gentleman, or a tyrant a kind and considerate friend. As insincerity characterizes the play throughout—as the tone of conversation is irreverent, skeptical of virtue and truth—as only one character is openly in favor of morality, prudence, and restraints, and he is attacked on every side—and as all the good that is done is accomplished by falsehood and deception—it would be useless to enter on a minute criticism of particular parts. After three careful readings the writer is unable to find any abstruse meaning to explain or counter work the obvious indelicacy of the plot and movement.

Don Cæzar de Bazan has less of profaneness in expression than many others, but more of licentiousness and treachery. The king is represented as making the most desperate efforts to violate his marriage vow, and much of the drama depends on the progress of the schemes which contribute to that end. *Don Cæzar de Bazan*, when he supposes that he is about to die, sings:—

> "Bright wine is the spell, boys, against every care,
> You'll find each delight that you seek is hid there;
> We topers ne'er think how the hours decline,
> When the glass of old Time runs smoothly with wine."

He calls himself a "poor," "dunned," "desperate libertine," and a well-known dramatic critic says, that "after we have said the best of him we can say, we must admit he is a desperate bully." This drama might with propriety be called the adventures of a desperate spendthrift, libertine, drunkard, and bully. Yet three English versions of it have been produced, and it has been very popular for more than a quarter of a century. Indeed, it is declared to be "a favorite entertainment in all the principal Theaters in the United States."

Masks and Faces is an attempt to show that actors and actresses are often better than their general reputation; but the spice of *Peg Woffington* is, that she did not act as she always had acted, and might reasonably be expected to act. The introduction of a "town rake" and an attempted seduction, the infatuation of *Vane*, and all the sentiments of the piece, except the benevolent relief of *Triplet* and the sympathy of *Woffington* with the heartbroken wife whose husband she had allured, are elements of a plot "which travels on the verge of open wickedness."

And here we conclude our strictures on particular plays. It would be easy to enlarge the number, and equally so to confirm the charges by the quotation of particular passages, but as it will be impossible for any one to truthfully deny the statements which we have made, it is as unnecessary as it would be unprofitable to transcribe the profane, indelicate, and corrupting expressions to these pages.

Some time since a statement, supported by what many would consider good authority, began its rounds through the newspapers, that, "with the exception of a few weeks of French *opéra bouffe* by a French company, not a New York Theater has, during one of the most successful seasons ever known, in any way whatever contributed to that vicious taste," etc., which a writer in some journal, being animadverted upon, "asserts must be pandered to in order that monetary success may be achieved."

This statement has one fatal defect. *It is not true.* Doubtless the author supposed it to be true. But during the season just closed more than one of the plays above described was brought out. Nevertheless, a paper professedly religious made an editorial on the above statement, and impliedly sanctioned the attendance of those who had formerly scrupled to go. A Christian matron, who had promised her children that they should go to the Theater whenever the stage became purified, read this misleading announcement, thought that the blessed time had fully come, brought her children to the city, and as soon as possible they went to one of the Theaters so highly commended, and gave all attention to the play. Soon the hero's character began to be unfolded, and he appeared to have sundry mistresses, and made attempts upon the virtue of other persons. The children needed no command to withdraw before the play concluded, but the mother, in conversation with a well-known literary gentleman of New York, who gave the writer these facts, expressed her regret that Christians should be imposed upon by such erroneous representations as those made in her "weekly religious paper."

The only key to the problem is, that the Theater forms the taste of its patrons, and that that taste excuses and even advocates what Christian morality condemns.

CHAPTER XVIII.

THE GREAT PLAYS OF SHAKSPEARE.

THE truth, naturalness, and grandeur of Shakspeare's plays, as a whole, need no eulogium from the present or any other writer. And an attack upon Shakspeare would be the most quixotic undertaking which could be attempted. Yet we confidently appeal to the judgment of those familiar with these wonderful works of dramatic art for confirmation of the observations which we now submit. These plays contain many obscene passages, and many that are profane; which passages were introduced by the author to suit the indelicacy of the age in which he lived, and were necessary to secure the interest and applause of the multitude. Many alterations have been made, and expurgated editions prepared for the stage, but it would not be possible for a woman to read them, as they are put upon the stage, before a promiscuous audience.

When Mrs. Kemble was reading in this country

it was truthfully said of her by an able critic, that she was "obliged to leap from point to point, from passage to passage, as one crossing a stream would leap from stone to stone in order to keep a dry foot."

It is the custom to make selections from Shakspeare for the use of boarding schools in the study of the language and of elocution, and a most judicious custom it is; but all will grant that it would be highly improper to take the plays *as they are*, and make them matters of criticism before a class of young ladies and gentlemen. But they are acted before them in the Theater; and the obscene and profane passages are not purified or redeemed by the magnificent and unobjectionable sentiments and expressions with which they are interwoven.

The argument made in defense of the lower order of plays, which are confessedly obscene, is this: "You like Shakspeare's plays; you think it no harm to see them?" The answer being in the affirmative, it is replied, "There are passages in Shakspeare as bad as any in the plays which you condemn;" and to that remark it can only be said, "In Shakspeare the objectionable features are not the bulk of the work." But the objectionable features are there, and in some of them they exist in such a shape that if Boucicault were to bring out a play containing as many objections of the same class as are produced in Shakspearean representations, he would be remorselessly condemned by many of the same critics who will call the writer a bigot, if not an "illiterate fanatic," for presuming to intimate that there is any thing in Shakspeare not proper to be uttered or acted in the presence of a promiscuous assembly, composed chiefly of young persons.

It is pertinent also to inquire what proportion of Shakspeare is presented in the Theater at the present time. The writer has excellent authority for saying that not more than one play in fifty performed in the Theaters of the principal cities of the country for the past ten years has been Shakspearean. And an estimate of the number of performances of the same piece will show that Shakspearean representations are too few, if they were unexceptionable, to modify the general charges against the Theater.

If five sixths of the plays presented are immoral in sentiment or expression, and indecent in manner, would it be gravely maintained that the acting of the "Pilgrim's Progress" once in every fifty nights would so redeem the whole institution as to make it proper for Christians to attend the Theater as a whole, and for youth to be encouraged to seek amusement there? It may be said, "We do not hold that it is right to see a vile play because the 'Pilgrim's Progress' is right, but we do hold that it is right to discriminate, and to see the 'Pilgrim's Progress.'" But the conclusive answer to this is, Not if by so doing you throw your whole influence in favor of an institution whose general effect is pernicious.

By putting your argument in that way you show that you ignore the duty of denying yourself for the sake of your Christian influence. The Theater is not to be judged as though representations were isolated things, like books. It is an *institution.* Reading has no significance in the way of moral influence. To say of a man, he reads, indicates nothing. To the limited circle who know *what* he reads the fact of his reading certain books has a moral meaning. But the Theater is an institution with a very pronounced character.

"Theater going" means *one thing* in the estimation of the public. He who goes to the Theater throws his influence in favor of the Theater as a whole. He may say, "I discriminate; I go to see Shakspeare;" but all who know him will say, "He goes to the Theater." It is here that the superficial character of the analogies sometimes drawn between going to the Theater and reading fiction may be seen. The attempt is made to compare an *institution* with isolated acts. If there were in all our cities large institutions known as "Recreation Halls," and in them gambling in all its forms, with many more degrading amusements, such as prize-fighting and drinking were allowed, and at the same time chess playing and other harmless games were practiced, and these last were in a very small proportion to the evil and sinful things done there, would it be proper for the Christian to patronize these "Recreation Halls," and say, "I ignore the gambling, and fighting, and drinking. I discriminate, and go there to play chess." It may be safely assumed that the very persons who profess to object to the average play, and argue in favor of going to the "Theater" to see "Shakspeare," would say of such a man, "Why does he not play chess at home, or give it up altogether? Why does he go to those 'Recreation Halls,' which are ruining so many?"

The sum of what the writer has tried to make clear in this chapter is, that though "Shakspeare's plays are the superbest of all plays," "there is many a dark spot of obscenity and profanation" upon them, which render many of them unfit to be performed before a promiscuous assembly, made up principally of youth; that if they were wholly unexceptionable they are too infrequently represented to redeem the general character of the Theater, which, as an institution, is evil; and that those who go to "see Shakspeare" furnish arguments for those who go to see plays every way inferior to Shakspeare's, and filled with the profaneness and obscenity, which are but incidents in his sublime compositions.

CHAPTER XIX.

CAN THE THEATER BE REFORMED?

THERE have always been persons who, while admitting existing evils, have held the opinion that the Theater can and should be reformed, and that the work of reconstructing it properly devolves on Christians. These are distinct propositions, and if the first were proved true, the second would not necessarily follow. Many reformations are demanded which the Christian can better promote, not by direct action upon the evils in question, but by disseminating and practicing the principles of the Gospel. As the outward symptoms and results of disease in the human body are to be removed, not by a direct attack, but by the general purification and restoration of the system, so many social evils and pernicious institutions may be destroyed or modified by the elevation of the moral tone of the community. Whether, then, Christians should undertake the reformation of the Theater by applying their energies directly to the task, is a question which would require cautious examination and discussion. But the primary inquiry is this: Is there any just reason to think that it is possible to reform the Theater? It is a very ancient institution, and its history runs through many nations and various stages of civilization. Is there any period in its history when it was in such a condition that the self-denying and devout Christian could consistently patronize it—when its characters, sentiments, expressions, attitudes, and accessories were such, that he who proposes for his rule of life, "Put ye on the Lord Jesus Christ, and make no provision for the flesh,"—he who sets his affections on things above, denying ungodliness and worldly lusts, "living soberly, righteously, and godly," could indulge in attendance upon it? "Cant! cant! unmitigated cant!" says some "Christian" who never thought of self-denial, or his influence over others as the regulating principle of his life. But where is the "cant?" Is it in the description of the Christian life, or in the historic statements concerning the Theater? That the spirit of the New Testament teaching is contained in those passages (not, indeed, with regard to the right kind and measure of amusement, but with respect to every thing evil) will hardly be doubted. The question, then, is, Where, in the long course of its history, has the Theater reached a development when it furnished suitable entertainment for Christians, and proper moral food for the undisciplined and plastic minds of youth. That isolated plays can be selected we concede, but they are as a few harmless or nutritious berries found in a wilderness of nightshade. The writer asks no mercy on the ground of ignorance if this characterization be not in the general true, for he has been at great pains to inform himself, and believes that the history of the Theater is correctly epitomized in the words of Pollock:—

> "The Theater was, from the very first,
> The favorite haunt of sin, though honest men,
> Some very honest, wise, and worthy men,
> Maintained it might be turned to good account;
> And so, perhaps, it might, but never was;
> From first to last it was an evil place."

We are not unaware of the fact that at certain periods the Drama was called, and in a sense was, the ally of the Church, but an examination of the Theater in those ages and countries, and of the religious condition of the Church at the same time, fully demonstrates the position here taken. It is not pretended that attendance on the Theater is inconsistent with the general moral and religious character of the average Roman Catholic population of the world, or with that of the Church of England in the times of Henry the Eighth, Edward, Elizabeth, or of Charles the First and his son. Nor is this a reflection upon the stricter part of those Churches, for we have in a former chapter pointed out the different views and practices found in them. The standard here assumed is not that which accommodates itself to those who "walk in the ways of their hearts and the sight of their eyes," but that which requires the nature to be adjusted to the law of God and the example of Christ, the standard which has been presented by all the "reformed" Churches, properly so called.

But is there any reason to hope for a reformation of that which has not, in so long a time and under such a variety of conditions, ever been in a state which did not need to be reformed? There is an almost insuperable obstacle in the way. The "classics" of the Drama are fixed, and by all the laws of art, and poetical, or dramatical composition, the generic character of the Theater is settled as firmly as the hills. And the iron grasp in which the "classics" hold the Theater is due alike to the veneration which is naturally given to antiquity, to the superior advantages which the "classic" writers had, and the vast intelligence which they possessed. And as in the case of inferior artists in any field, beauties are feebly imitated, while faults are easily copied and intensified. A divergence so great as would be necessary to render the Theater no longer obnoxious to Christian condemnation could not be brought about in many ages unless all the laws which have obtained in other departments of progress should fail. The rise of a transcendent genius, such as Shakspeare, to whose ability should be added the virtues and tastes adequate to revolutionize the Theater and the Theater-going public, is not to be anticipated, and nothing less than this could effect the result.

Another difficulty inheres in the demand for excitement, and in the impossibility of producing it without the delineation of vice and all its attendant entanglements, whether in tragedy or comedy. This remark having been elaborated in a preceding chapter, nothing more than a reference to it here is necessary. Those who fancy that the just representation of human life, in which "praise or censure are awarded according to the principles of Christian morality,"—in which evangelical godliness is always praised and the want of it deplored,—can afford permanent amusement to the general public, are under a delusion as great as was poor Miss Bacon when she believed that she had proved as clearly as a demonstration in Euclid, that Lord Bacon wrote Shakspeare to introduce a philosophy for which the world was not ready.

CHAPTER XX.

CAN THE THEATER BE REFORMED?—CONTINUED.

THE improbability, if not the impossibility, of the Theater's being reformed, appears from the relation which its patrons sustain to the character of the entertainment furnished. While a higher function may be claimed for the Drama than providing amusement, it will not be questioned that the Theater is supported by the bulk of its patrons as an entertainment. And as the management must make a financial success, it is plain that the representations cannot diverge very far from the tastes of the majority. If the attempt be made to force them to hear something above their intellectual or moral level, it must be "floated" by something at or below that level. The money of the most depraved attendant bears the same relation to the sum total as an equal amount paid by the most refined. If, then, nine tenths of the Theater-going public call for the present order of plays they will get what they call for, or the management will fail. Garrick understood this, and admitted it in the well-known epilogue which he delivered at the opening of the Drury Lane Theater in the city of London :—

> " Hard is his lot, that here by fortune placed
> Must watch the wild vicissitudes of taste ;
> With ev'ry meteor of caprice must play,
> And chase the new-born bubbles of the day.
> Ah ! let not censure term our fate our choice,
> The stage but echoes back the public voice ;
> The *drama's laws* the *drama's patrons give*,
> For we that *live to please* must *please* to live."

One hundred and twenty-eight years have passed since that epilogue, composed by Dr. Johnson, was spoken by Garrick, and it closed with the following earnest appeal :—

> " Then prompt no more the follies you decry,
> As tyrants doom their tools of guilt to die ;
> 'Tis yours this night to bid the reign commence
> Of rescued nature and reviving sense ;
> To chase the charms of sound, the pomp of show,
> For useful mirth and salutary woe ;
> Bid scenic virtue form the rising age,
> And truth diffuse her radiance from the stage."

But during that long period the " drama's laws " have been given by the " drama's patrons," and the

Theater in New York is in some respects, though not in all, below what it was then, and in none very much better. The prospects of a reformation of the Theater, as deduced from the fact that "the stage but echoes back the public voice," and also from the tastes of the bulk of its patrons as evinced by the kind of pieces that have the "greatest run," is as remote as ever.

We may see, also, that there is no probability of the Theater's being reformed from within itself. To say nothing of the fact just urged, that no considerable portion of its supporters demand a reformation, there is no reason to expect, from the moral convictions of the composers and actors of the present day, any improved standard of matter or manner. Let it not be supposed that this is an insinuation against the moral character of actors in the ordinary sense of that term: that is a question which the writer does not think of much importance to a calm examination of the subject. What is meant is, that neither actors nor composers look at the subject from the *Christian point of view*, or have any sympathy with the strictness of life required in the New Testament. If they have any affiliation with Christians it is rather with what may be called the "cavalier" type. We have, indeed, heard of an actress who is endeavoring to blend a religious life with appearances in most licentious plays; but an abnormal instance is of no value on the general question. We presume that it will not be pretended that there is any error in our statement on this subject.

But in addition, we must say that whatever may be their private moral character, good, bad, or indifferent, on this question of what is right in Theatrical representation, there seems to be in them all a "strange obliquity of vision." A recent instance is furnished by a lady of fine literary abilities and reputation who has recently entered the dramatic profession, and comes forward over her own signature in the paper to which she has long been a brilliant contributor, to defend the Theater and repel attacks upon it. Her testimony is valuable, and her mode of viewing the question is that of the profession at large. Says Miss Kate Field, in the "New York Tribune" of March 29, 1875: "As a rule managers prefer legitimate plays acted by ladies and gentlemen. If such do not pay, they spread the viands in demand." This is confirmatory of Garrick, as before quoted, and authorizes us to conclude the nature of the demand from the "viands spread." "Many a time I have heard managers deplore the uneducated taste of their audiences, and regret the necessity of acting down to their level." But, alas! the fatal necessity exists. She proceeds: "But it is a mistake to suppose the public depraved; it is a mistake to declare that under all circumstances the *Black Crook* will draw better than *Richard III.* Let *Richard III.* be as well acted throughout as the *Black Crook* was illustrated, and Shakspeare will win a decided victory. It is the absence of dramatic ability that renders Shakspeare unattractive. The most cultivated public had rather see beautiful dancing and scenery than a great dramatist murdered." The writer is aware that these passages are somewhat contradictory, but as that is not considered a defect in style in these days, he quotes them that the testimony may be weighed by those who have not seen the original article. The two explanations are, first, that of the management that they must act down to the level; and, second, absence of dramatic ability in the actors, which drives even the cultivated to lower exhibitions.

To our amazement we find this brilliant lady offering a defense of the *Black Crook;* and in that defense, "the way of looking at the subjects," which precludes all hope of reformation from within the Theatrical profession, is convincingly and sadly illustrated.

"The *Black Crook* was complete in its way. Its way is not intellectual. It is sensuous; but unless people are vile at heart, and seek in such spectacles food for vice, even the greatly abused *Black Crook* needs do no harm. There are those who are shocked at marble Venuses and Greek slaves. Others see in them perfect form, and thank the creator for the existence of so much beauty."

Let the intelligent Christian reader ponder that passage well. It implies the purity of character for which its author is held in such high esteem by so wide a circle of friends and admirers. But what a view of this subject it gives! "Unless people are vile at heart, and seek in such spectacles food for vice, it needs do no harm." But this is only to say that a pious city missionary could visit dens of infamy without being contaminated. The average public, the youth, who throng to see these spectacles" "are not more vile at heart" than mankind at large; but *all have passions* whose restraint in thought and feeling, as well as in act, is a solemn Christian duty. And though they may not consciously seek food for vice, the influence of such spectacles on the common mind is harmful, while to those who do go to seek food for vice every facility is offered.

The analogy between Greek slaves and marble Venuses, and the *Black Crook*, is strangely inappropriate. "The Greek slaves and marble Venuses" are *dead marble*. Would any one defend a class of exhibitions once common, but now prohibited by law, on the ground that unless persons were vile at heart, and seek food for vice, they need do no harm? But we pursue this subject no further, except to say that there is no hope of the Theater's being reformed by the profession, who have no sympathy with the Christian view of life, morals, and religion, and look at the subject from a point of view so remote that they *cannot see what is needed.*

It now only remains to inquire whether the Theater can be reformed from without; that is, can Christian poets and moralists be found to compose, and Christian men and women to represent, their compositions in living sympathy with their work. And this is one of a large class of inquiries which, when propounded, answer themselves, and in this case the answer is in the negative.

Such an attempt would have many insuperable obstacles to surmount. Dramatic poets are not made to order, and actors, whatever their natural endowments, require long training and practice before they can succeed. Such a movement would, of necessity, avow hostility to the existing institution, and could find no materials on which to rely. The existing literature of the stage could be but in small part appropriated. The dullness of "Christian" acting, and "Christian" comedy and tragedy, could not compete before the Theater-going public with the high seasoning to which they have so long been accustomed, while those who should begin to attend for the first time would be acting from principle in the line of penance, and the "beggarly array of empty boxes" which would soon be seen, would furnish boundless material for satire.

It must not be lost sight of that in every case the number of Christian Theater-goers would be much smaller in proportion to their whole number than of irreligious persons. For every active Christian has a demand upon him for from two to three evenings per week: such as the prayer-meeting; if he happens to be an officer, the official meeting; the meeting of the Sunday-school teachers; and many other calls upon his time. So that very many Christians, if they loved the Theater, and if the Utopian Reformed Theater were perfected, could not often patronize it. And very many pious men and women find in their religious exercises all the enjoyment they need, and are cheerful through life without once thinking of the necessity of making systematic provision for amusement. Others, and in the aggregate a great multitude of Christians, are poor, and to educate their children, and to give a little to Christian benevolence, requires all that they can save, and they could have no money for such amusements. Hence, it is equally chimerical to expect that the Theater can be reformed by Christians either from without, or by their holding, through numbers, the balance of power and becoming the arbiters of taste.

The suggestion is made by Miss Field that, "were enlightened souls to endow a Theater, as colleges are frequently endowed, whereby it might become totally independent of popular caprice, the benefits conferred on public morals and on histrionic art would be incalculable. Is the suggestion utterly Utopian?"

If the benefit to public morals of such an institution would be incalculable, it is, perhaps, a valid inference that the influence on the public morals of the present condition of the Theater is very bad; but however this may be, the radical difference between colleges and places of amusement must not be overlooked. Colleges make no appeal to the general public, but to a particular class, having a careful preparation, a definite purpose, and a willingness to be trained by those whose authority and competency are recognized. But an endowed Theater would either open its doors to the public for free admission, or make the usual charge.

In the former case it would be subject to the charge of being hostile to the regular profession, and in the latter it would not be removed from popular caprice, and in any form it would be subject to criticism and intense competition. And if Christians were to attempt a censorship of such a Theater, or any other, it would be a mark for every shaft of ridicule; and from causes heretofore set forth, and the absence of the usual excitement, it would be an insipid and unsatisfactory thing. But it is unnecessary to further discuss an impracticable proposition.

CHAPTER XXI.

MAKING UP JUDGMENT ON THE MAIN ISSUE.

CERTAIN remarkable coincidences must strike every one in reviewing this subject. In general terms it may be said that all evangelical Churches in this country, except the Protestant Episcopal, are opposed to the Theater, and teach that it should not be attended by Christians: and that the more in sympathy with spiritual religion the ministers and members of that Church are, the less the countenance they give to the Theater. It is equally obvious that all the non-evangelical bodies are either favorable or indifferent in their moral attitude to the Theater; also that the more worldly and formal portion of the Protestant Episcopal Church entertain no scruples against the Theater, and generally attend it.

While the more earnest and devoted to the work of promoting Christianity by personal efforts any denomination may be, the more pronounced is its hostility to the Theater. In all the Churches those ministers most distinguished for piety, most zealous in self-denying labors, and most successful in genuine revivals of religion, are most opposed to the Theater; while those notoriously indolent, luxurious, and tolerant to worldliness, with few exceptions, furnish ministerial apologists for the Theater.

It is not affirmed that all who denounce the Theater are eminent for zeal and piety, or that all worldly-minded ministers apologize for the Theater. Men may have just views of one subject, and be very inconsistent in their opinions and practices on others; and often persons are very loose in their views and indefensible in their general conduct, and yet, on a particular topic, they are correct. The general representation here given has as few exceptions as any statement concerning human character and conduct could have.

In local Churches, where the members in general give themselves up to Theater-going and kindred amusements, spiritual power declines to the lowest ebb, revivals are unknown, and conversions are rare, and mostly among children. In particular Churches, whatever may have been their past history, whenever a genuine, wide-spread, and powerful revival of personal religion takes place, the people spontaneously renounce the Theater, and no instance can be assigned of such a revival occurring in any Church contemporaneously with a general attendance of its members and congregation on the Theater.

What is the key to these coincidences? How have the Churches and ministers been led to this unanimity of sentiment? The solution of the problem is in the character and influence of the Theater, and especially its effect on the young. Those who have made it their chief business to promote the spirituality of Christ's Church, have been as naturally led to inquire into the influence of the Theater as physicians have been led to ascertain the effects of malaria on the physical system; and the almost absolute concurrence of opinion furnishes a presumption which scarcely needs the confirmation of independent examination. Those who advance boldly upon the world in the hope of bringing it to Christ, are obliged to contend with opposing influences; and they see that few things are more unfavorable to religion than the practice of Theater-going, and that nothing is more potent in causing men to relinquish a strictly religious life than the spirit and associations of the Theater. And these deadening effects of Theater-going on Churches must have a cause, and that cause cannot but be in the character of the Theater itself, while the indulgence shown to the institution by non-evangelical bodies, and professedly irreligious or atheistical writers and teachers, should not surprise any who consider their general scheme of religion and character.

The position proper to be taken by all Christian ministers and conscientious Christians, if the principles here advanced are true, and the statements made are facts, is *opposition to the Theater*, classing it with the "unfruitful works of darkness" with which we are to have "no fellowship." This opposition should be *open, candid,* and *uncompromising*. Whoever avows such an opposition will himself be opposed by the self-styled "liberals" of every grade, who will sneer at his bigotry and narrowness. He will be opposed by a very few good men who differ in judgment on this question from the rest of the Church. He will be opposed by all who are attempting the impossible, and, from the New Testament point of view, the *perfidious* task of attempting to harmonize Christianity and worldliness. He will, perhaps, be satirized by the secular press, and denounced as a Pharisee by many nominal professors, and regarded by not a few undiscerning youth as an enemy to innocent enjoyment.

But what one thing can a minister do to promote the cause of Christ which will not expose him to opposition? And the opposition he provokes is sometimes a proof of the power of his ministry. Paul thanked God that a great and effectual door was opened to him, and there were "many adversaries." The present is no time for compromise on this or any other question. There is an appalling disintegration of morals. There is nothing gained by compromise. To be called a bigot or a fanatic by the opponents of religion is a price to be paid for true success. The fawning of those whose worldliness has been flattered is as disgusting to the soul of every *man* as decayed fruit is to his taste.

"But some of our wealthiest members attend the Theater, and if we speak too plainly they will become disaffected and leave." But many of our wealthiest men are the truest in their devotion to our principles, and more would be if their pastors were faithful to them. But suppose that a few should leave your Church because you have done right! Which is the healthier, a tree pruned of dead and decaying branches, or one in which decay is going on unchecked? If any one will leave the Baptist, the Presbyterian, the Congregational, or the Methodist Episcopal Church, because you, its pastor, endeavor to dissuade the youth from the Theater, give him any credentials to which, after the development of such a spirit, he may be entitled, and rejoice that the Lord is giving you such a seal to your ministry. But very few will depart if your zeal is "according to knowledge," and your testimony on this subject is delivered at the right *time*, in the right *way*, and in the right *spirit*.

CHAPTER XXII.

HOW TO PRESENT THIS SUBJECT.

THE suggestions made in this chapter are presented with some confidence, and have arisen from much consideration of the subject, from conversations with discriminating pastors of different denominations, intelligent parents and teachers, as well as from some years of experiment in endeavoring to counteract the tendency to Theater-going among professed Christians. The principle of primary importance is to endeavor to raise such a high standard of spirituality and Christian refinement that those to whom we preach will have no relish for such an amusement, and, consequently, no desire to go to the Theater.

While recognizing fully the compatibility of a due proportion of recreative amusement with the highest religious attainments, the writer has no doubt that the more rationally religious a person is, the less he feels the need of amusement as such, and the greater his distaste for every questionable form thereof. Such a Christian does not begin his inquiries by that common but most misleading question, "What harm is there in it?" but asks, "What good is there in it?" and, if this cannot be definitely answered, can easily find ways of gratifying and recreating himself without hazarding uncertain experiments. "And be not drunk with wine, wherein is excess; but be filled with the Spirit; speaking to yourselves in psalms and hymns and spiritual songs, singing and making melody in your heart to the Lord." This inspired direction teaches us that the Christian must not resort to wine nor any other pernicious thing to keep up his spirits; and while it does not teach that all manifestations and causes of joy except singing psalms are wrong, it certainly implies a state in which the character will be so independent of merely worldly sources as to admit of the exercise of a wise discrimination. Persons without religion, or with only enough conviction of truth to perpetuate an uneasy and an accusing conscience, *must have* very frequent and absorbing amusements to smother their disquietude and misery; but it is not a *want of happiness* that drives the growing Christian to it. Relaxation and rest, and the necessity of variety of occupation to health and elasticity, are the occasions which he finds for diversion. If, then, the general effect of preaching be to promote genuine religion and real "growth in grace," it diminishes the passion for amusement, and destroys the taste for all questionable kinds; while he who thus "enjoys" religion is willing to make any sacrifice for the good of others.

Some pastors have had so high an opinion of this principle as to rely on it entirely, and have said nothing against intemperance, fraud, gaming, or Sabbath-breaking. But this is not enough, for Satan often comes as an "angel of light." As in the case of the human constitution we must not only observe the general laws of health, but also be vigilant to discern and check the insidious encroachments of disease, so we must not only teach positive truth, but we must lay bare the forms in which evil enters the individual life and pollutes the Church. At this stage, however, several errors may be made, whose influence, if they are committed by the pastor, will weaken him before the people. Indiscriminate denunciation is very common and works no good. "No Christian ever went to the theater." "No Christian ever wanted to go." "To wish to go is a certain sign of an unregenerate state." "All who do go to the theater are low characters, drunkards, prostitutes, gamblers, and such like."

These statements cannot be maintained. They are false, and people know that they are false. It may be that the youth to whom you preach have worthy relatives, perhaps parents, who sometimes, even frequently, go. When such statements are made these youth are driven either to disbelieve the statement, or class these relatives and friends with corrupt characters. The latter they will not do, hence they conclude that the minister is a bigot, or does not know what he is talking about. Thence it is a short distance to the conclusion that the Theater is not very bad, and that the Church is an intolerable burden, and religion a gloomy thing for the youth. Nor is this all; confidence in the minister's reliability is permanently and generally weakened.

The use of personalities and epithets on this, as

on all other subjects, should be avoided. To introduce side issues and raise questions which can never be disposed of is also an unwise method of procedure. That "all actors and actresses are corrupt" cannot be proved. It is sufficient to assume—what can be proved—that there is no sympathy, and never has been any, between members of this profession and evangelical piety; and that the tendency of their profession is the explanation of that fact. It may further be shown that the domestic relations of actors and actresses have, in very many instances, exhibited the freedom which they so often illustrate on the stage. But this is very different from making a general statement that "all actors and actresses are flagrantly immoral."

Another grave error is the waiting for a crisis to denounce the Theater. The Rev. Mr. A. was a pastor in N. For nine years he said nothing about the Theater in public or private. On a certain occasion he heard that Mr. B., one of his leading members, had been at the Theater in New York, and taken his family. On the following Sunday he delivered a terrible tirade against the Theater, said that he would "bear his testimony" that "men and devils could not padlock his lips," lashed himself into a tempest of fury, created a great excitement in the town, advertising the fault of the brother to *whom he had never spoken privately on the subject.* This course was neither judicious nor courageous. To declaim at a man from the safe retreat of a pulpit is not to do as valiantly as to approach him first privately in the "spirit of meekness;" and to complicate the discussion of a subject such as this with intense personal feeling, is the depth of folly. To make a martyr of a man is a good way of causing all his friends to defend his conduct, and to give all who agree with him on the matter an effective weapon to use for their own purposes. The true method is to set forth your views on the Theater clearly, forcibly, proportionately, uncompromisingly, in the *regular course* of religious instruction. If you do this the crisis may never come. If it should come, it may not be a great crisis. If it should prove a great crisis do not shrink from it, for your regular teaching will have raised up a phalanx to support you. The winds strengthen a tree whose roots are strong, and deep, and far-reaching, but they tear up those which have little depth of earth.

Thus far we have considered the discussion of the subject by the pastor in the pulpit. It is, or ought to be, hardly necessary to say that he must be at all times ready to defend his sentiments in private, and must *act in harmony with them.* He who is silent when his friends advance sentiments which he believes dangerous, or utters a mild demurrer, unsupported either by fact or argument, can do but little by public appeals. And the minister who admits that "he visited the Theater when he was abroad," or moves among his people regretting "that it will not do for him to hear Ristori," need not be surprised if those who hear him speak thus attend the Theater instead of the prayer-meeting; and also, if they seem to have some contempt for a man who either has no opinions, or lacks the courage to defend them, or to act in harmony with them. We would not be supposed to mean that a minister must carry a tomahawk and scalping-knife with him, attacking, on this or any other subject, his parishioners; but we do mean that he should at all proper times, in a gentlemanly manner, explain and vindicate his views.

In arguing with young Christians, whose sentiments are not yet fully formed, the most effective method is to appeal to them on the ground of their influence. To show them that they cannot consistently remain connected with the Church and attend the Theater; that if they do so, many of their brethren and sisters will be grieved; that they will have no moral influence over their irreligious friends, who can never be impressed with the need of religion so long as those who profess it are not distinguished from the world. If they say that some will be alienated from religion by their narrowness if they refuse to accompany them to the Theater, let them be shown that the *world in general count that an advantage* is gained over the Christian who is seen at the Theater; and that it is better to be true to Christ at the expense of temporary alienation, than to acquiesce, in the vain hope that compromising with evil will attract the irreligious to Christ.

Persons seldom refuse to become Christians *merely* because they think it a yoke, but because they love the world; and few are the cases in which by investigation *previous to repentance* they have reconsidered the matter and concluded that it is not a yoke. In addition it may be shown them, that he who earnestly prays, "Lead us not into temptation," cannot consistently put himself in its way.

Parents have it in their power to fix the sentiments of their children on this subject, not by creating an unreasoning prejudice, but by informing them of the solid grounds of their objections. They can also control their conduct by parental authority until they can reason. Some parents have tried the hazardous plan of taking their children once or twice "to show them the folly of it." Which will they be more likely to remember, the protest of their parents, or the fascination of the spectacle? It would hardly be wise to give a boy a few bottles of champagne that he may "see the folly of drinking." Nor would the folly of going to the Theater be at once apparent to an ordinary youth; in which, as we have seen, much of the danger consists, that improper sentiments and forms of expression will be imperceptibly imbibed, the imagination filled with unhealthy ideas, and the passions prematurely aroused and morbidly excited.

We sometimes find parents who say that they were brought up too strictly, and that they intend to indulge their children. Granting that they were brought up too strictly, which in many alleged instances is not true, the reaction too often leads them to indulge their children to a ruinous extent; and thus far the careers of these indulged children are not very encouraging in a religious way, and sometimes not as respects ordinary morality.

Doubtless, in former times, many parents were too strict. But this strictness consisted in the tyrannical oppressiveness of their manner, and the absence of all reasonable explanation of their commands, as well as in forbidding innocent pleasures. But those parents who prohibit Theater-going, and explain the reason for the prohibition as soon as the child can understand it, at the same time showing a lively interest in every unobjectionable amusement, will be increasingly honored for it to the end of their lives. It is true that while the minds of children are undeveloped, they will "think" as children, "speak" as children, and "understand" as children; and much firmness will be required to suppress their burning desires to see every thing of which they hear; but the difficulty is no greater in this than in many other questions in which the matured judgment of parents differs from the unwise opinions of children. The capricious smile of an indulged and spoiled child is not to be compared as a source of consolation to the intelligent Christian parent, with the approbation which well-trained sons or daughters will give when in after years they rise up and call their parents blessed." And in endeavoring to avoid undue strictness, it is no more necessary to become unduly indulgent than it is to commit suicide by gluttony to avoid death by starvation.

CHAPTER XXIII.

A HEALTHY AND HAPPY RELIGIOUS LIFE.

TWO extreme views have been held of the subject of religion, and the tendency of mankind has been to oscillate between them, never remaining long at the center, where reposes the truth in its symmetry and beauty, awaiting the embrace of all who will tarry long enough to perceive its attractions. By some in all ages, and by most in particular periods, all conversation and reading not of a directly devotional or religious character has been considered sinful; business has been regarded as a necessary evil; every form of recreation dangerous and useless; the ardent love of nature a suspicious indication; society a hot-bed of temptation. Religion, in their view, consisted chiefly in self-denial, solitude, and the preservation of a solemn and even awful sense of eternal things, which covered life with a funereal gloom. The love of art, music, and beauty is vanity; and fasting, vigils, and directly spiritual employments "the whole duty of man." This view of religion has flourished chiefly in the Church of Rome among the monkish orders and brother and sisterhoods. But it has also affected Protestantism, sometimes giving character to entire sects; and whenever the Church in general has become worldly, a reaction has set in which has tended to this extreme, its progress thitherward having been accelerated by the persecution and opposition which good men have encountered.

The irrationality, however, of this view, in its most pronounced form, is clear. It is a disparagement of the universe which God has made, and it is injurious to health, shortening and often destroying life. It is essentially morbid, and distorts the mind and heart, unbalancing the entire nature. It is modeled on the practice of John the Baptist, and not on the teachings or practice of Christ.

In our time, however, there is but little need of protesting against this extreme, for we live in "a time of transition." Many would reduce the religious life to a few public services, and these must be made interesting by outward and sensuous things;

as music, flowers, and variety. So that, in many services, the elements least regarded are the word of God and spirit of devotion. Self-denial is ignored, and self-gratification substituted. Solemn thinking is an intolerable burden, anxiety for the spiritual condition of others is not promoted, and vigorous efforts to induce them to enter the service of Christ are seldom or never made. Material gratification—accumulation of wealth—is the ruling principle with most adults, while the real pleasure of most youth is found in display, worldliness, and questionable or positively harmful amusements: these, all the while, fancying that Jesus is the Saviour of the world, and that they will at last "get to heaven," of which, however, their ideas are vague—some depicting it to themselves as a place of rest, others as a family re-union, and most as a kind of "Central Park" in the universe, where the inhabitants will never be sick, or poor, or disappointed, and will listen to music, and have every thing that they want. Of the root ideas of the heaven promised in the New Testament—spiritual purity, the love, and knowledge, and presence of God, and the fellowship of Christ—they never think, for "where the treasure is there will the heart be also."

Whoever will read the New Testament will see that this view of the life of piety is even more irrational than the other. That was serious, this is frivolous; that considered sin a deadly foe and fought against it; this, as a pleasant companion to be watched but toyed with, and, perhaps, embraced; that did good very often by its terribly earnest labors for the salvation of men, this does nothing but carelessly sow dead seed; that kept alive a sense of the reality of religion, this turns it into a melo-drama. This is the extreme prevalent in this age; and we have apostles of license instead of liberty, who are applauded by admiring friends in proportion to the skill and boldness with which they reduce religion to sentimentality, and put the conscience to sleep while the life is one of worldliness and frivolity. Into such a religion as this Theater-going, Sabbath excursions, wine and card parties, fit very easily. There is a correspondence between the inward state and the outward life; but when the heart is filled with love to God, and really devoted to Christ, an unendurable discord between such things and the inner life is apparent.

A healthy and happy religious life avoids these extremes. Its possessor fears God but is not afraid of him, loves him but also reveres him, confides fully in him but has respect to the condition on which his promises are made. He begins and ends the day with earnest secret prayer; and whenever conscious of needing special help, guidance, or comfort, he calls upon God. The public services of the sanctuary are delightful to him, and he is always strengthened and encouraged by the communion of saints and the worship of God. He aims to be a genuine philanthropist, ever ready to aid others, and is as anxious to confer spiritual benefits upon them as to relieve their physical necessities. He attends strictly to business, but, regarding it as a means to an end, does not become its slave. Social intercourse is pleasant to him, and his moral and spiritual instincts lead him to select the refined, the intelligent, the pure, instead of the coarse or corrupt. All physical and sensuous gratifications are enjoyed in their place and proportion, and kept in due subordination. He indulges in nothing pernicious, in nothing that violates the precepts of Christ, that injures others, or destroys his influence as a Christian. And he is ready, at the proper time, for special labors in the Church to promote the conversion of men. Naturally a youth will give more time to pleasure and society than a man in the prime of life, who will be more closely occupied with the cares of business; while the aged should cultivate a quiet and contemplative spirit as the great change approaches.

This healthy and happy religious life is not morbid, because not disproportionate. It develops man symmetrically, admits of the greatest happiness, and introduces no elements of misery. It gives the greatest influence for good, and is the religion of Christ and his apostles. But it is impossible to graft Theater-going upon it without destroying the original stock. For Theater-going, as a habit and for the love of it, implies either inactivity or dullness of the conscience, else the spectator would be pained by every element of immorality and irreligion. While he who returns from an average play will hardly *pray*, even if he takes the time to "say his prayers;" and a willingness to be delighted by the progress of such events and characters as are delineated in the Theater implies such an easy view of human nature in general that no motives will exist to prompt to special efforts to lead men to repentance. He who can laugh at sin or a sinful character will never feel an agony of soul to save the sinner.

If it be said that there are persons who "love the '*Black Crook*' and yet are zealous members of Churches, laboring to save men," it is replied that they are so few that they must be classed with other unnatural instances which shed no light on the tendency of influences. But it will hardly be found that such persons have any heart for private, personal, earnest expostulations; their zeal usually evaporates in singing, speaking, and praying in public, while the texture of their general religious character is defective.

Thus have we tried to show why it is that he who attempts to find a place in his religious life for Theater-going hazards the destruction of its purity, and consistency, and power. Nor does he lose any thing of value if he renounces the Theater forever. For the more closely we examine the acts of self-denial required of the Christian, the more obvious it becomes that those which are demanded by our personal necessities in the religious life, bear the same relation to our growth that pruning does to the growth and fruit-bearing qualities of a tree: therefore Christ said, "Every branch in me that beareth not fruit he [the Father] taketh away: and every branch that beareth fruit, he purgeth it, that it may bring forth more fruit:" while those acts of self-denial required by our relation to others pertain to superfluities, and rarely or never to any thing of really great importance.

CHAPTER XXIV.

THE OPEN FIELD OF CHRISTIAN PRIVILEGE.

WE are sometimes told that if the Church prohibits the Theater it should furnish a substitute. This requirement has a plausible sound, but nothing more. The function of the Church is not to map out the whole sphere of possible activity and erect at every turn sign-boards warning individuals away from certain points, and at the same time indicating just what walks may be permitted. Nor is the individual Christian to be treated as an imbecile, but as a rational and responsible being. "Prove all things: hold fast that which is good. Abstain from all appearance of evil," or as some think it should be rendered, "from every form of evil," are not only commands, but constitute the great charter of Christian liberty. It is to be presumed that if the Church protests against intemperance, that the Christian who practices temperance will not need to have a substitute furnished to him for the stimulus of the intoxicating cup. All nature furnishes wholesome food, opportunities for healthful exercise and rest, the pure and invigorating air, and the sparkling water, or the "cup which cheers but does not inebriate."

Let the temperate man govern himself by the laws of his God, and the constitution which he has given him, and he will need no specific directions from the Church. So when Christianity prohibits particular acts of dishonesty the reformed swindler has the whole field of legitimate effort in which to obtain an honest livelihood. And when the Christian Church endeavors to persuade its members to abstain from evil and destructive amusements, is it to be told that it must find a substitute? All varieties of innocent recreation are before the Christian; let him exclaim, in the language of David, "I will walk at liberty: for I seek thy precepts." Nevertheless it may be well to show how utterly unnecessary the Theater as an amusement is to any Christian. Multitudes of the best, purest, wisest, most refined persons of both sexes never entered a Theater in their lives. Many of the most hopeful, cheerful, and happy people have never laughed at lewd wit, profaneness, or exceptionable sentiments in the Theater, for they have never entered its doors. Many have at certain periods attended the Theater, but have subsequently conscientiously remained away, and have not lost their cheerfulness. And why should any think that no substitute can be found for the Theater? For all that is good in it, many substitutes can be found; for *what is bad* no substitute *in kind* can be asked by the Christian. But it may be said, "We ask not for ourselves but for our children." Is it so? Have you, then, ever seriously tried to amuse them? At home, by free and familiar intercourse, by conversation, by narrative, by always looking for incidents to interest them? By inculcating a taste for reading, and furnishing them with new and interesting books, papers, magazines, and objects of interest of every kind? by encouraging reading aloud, and doing all in your power to make the evenings interesting? Have you encouraged them to learn to sing, or to play on musical instruments, and thus provided the materials for an amateur musical entertainment at home? As an amusement, a means of promoting cheerfulness, a refining influence, a cementing bond, increasing parental and filial and brotherly affection, and as a friend to good health, the cultivation of social and instrumental music in the family circle is invaluable. Then there are for little children countless games which the ingenuity of all lands and ages has invented and commerce brings to your door; while for youth there are all games that are not intrinsically demoralizing or by their associations made dangerous. Company, also, when discreetly managed, may be made to furnish the materials of a great variety of amusement. The occasional invitation of suitable young people who, when properly trained, need but little supervision, with moderate refreshments and early departure; the bringing forward of all but the youngest children when general entertainments are given; and the selection for guests of persons of refinement, of travelers, of those who pursue professions and kinds of business which qualify them to narrate interesting and exciting adventures, experiments, etc., of fine singers and readers, will give endless delight to your children. But "you have never thought of these things." What have you done? Have you neglected your family? caused your sons and daughters to think that you were annoyed by them; made the boys feel that their parents were never so glad as when they were in bed or out of doors? Perhaps if you would give a little attention to these things they might think the home evenings were the pleasantest in the year. But there are many admirable amusements to be enjoyed away from home, such as riding, for those who can afford it; walking for those who know how to do it, and excursions of various kinds: the visiting of museums and art galleries, of public institutions, and all the entertainments provided by academies, Sunday-schools, congregations, Young Men's Christian Associations, etc. There are grand musical entertainments, magnificent concerts, which, if you allow your children to attend two or three of them in a season, will form their taste and give them increasing pleasure as well as something to anticipate and recollect with delight. There are lecturers of all kinds to be heard, and not a few who are almost comedians, but, being held responsible for their matter as well as manner, are not likely to offend good morals, however much they may violate good taste.

Nor should the magicians and ventriloquists be forgotten, who afford infinite sport to children, and are some of them worthy of patronage by thoughtful people whom they will teach a needed lesson, namely, that the senses are not to be implicitly relied on when they appear to contradict the general sense of mankind.

The brilliant scientific lectures attended by thrilling experiments which are now put within the reach even of the poor in our large cities, combine instruction and amusement in such harmonious proportions that the best possible effects are obtained. With such a programme as the Young Men's Christian Associations in the principal cities offer to young people of limited means, none need ask, "What shall I do if I cannot go to the Theater?" While for *persons of wealth* to affirm that they cannot amuse themselves and their children without the aid of the Theater is to stigmatize themselves as deficient in candor, or as below mediocrity in intelligence.

The foregoing is not presented as a full description of the wide field of innocent amusement, but as a general outline of it. To some it may seem like a desert of sand. But as the purest spring water seems insipid to the man whose taste has been corrupted by drunkenness, so to the habitual Theater-goer of average intelligence every thing but the Theater will be very tame.

CHAPTER XXV.

CONCLUSION.

WITH this chapter we conclude our survey of this practical and important subject. "Lovers of pleasures more than lovers of God" may feel unmeasured contempt for the work, and, perhaps, for the author. But even they, if conscious of their moral condition and attitude toward the question, must admit that their feelings, if they are excited by the doctrines taught, but confirm the truthfulness of the teaching. And they must see that it would be impossible to treat any subject fairly, and at the same time "conciliate those who are determined not to be conciliated." We incur a similar liability to contempt whenever we urge any of the more humbling doctrines of Christianity, and any of the more irksome duties of the Christian life. But to support us under contempt in this instance we have the consciousness of our own sincerity, the concurrent judgment of the most active and spiritually-minded ministers and members of all Churches, and the *certainty* that *any one who may be led by our book* to *renounce* the *Theater*, or be *confirmed* in *his opposition* to it, will never have reason to think that *we have weakened* his *faith* or *diminished* his *usefulness* as a Christian, or *imperiled his hope of heaven.*

Some worthy persons may dissent from our general conclusion. This will neither surprise nor discourage us, for the most approved and necessary truths do not receive universal assent. Many never did, and never will, investigate this or any other question. They are governed by impulse, fancy, prepossession, or prejudice, and employ their reasoning faculties, not in coming to a conclusion, but in fortifying, defending, or illustrating an opinion which they adopted in the beginning without consideration. Therefore, if our reasoning be correct and our conclusions just, we cannot reasonably expect to convince all. Besides such as have just been characterized, there may be a few persons of ability and piety who will examine this subject and come to an opposite conclusion. In most of these cases, however, the explanation of their differing from so vast a majority of Christian men of all creeds is this: They fall into the error of estimating the effect of the Theater upon others by its supposed effect upon themselves.

A disciplined Christian, though he would not voluntarily read, or hear, or see that which is evil, may, indeed, assimilate the good and reject the evil in the books he reads, and in what he sees or hears; but youth, though innocent of evil intent, have not this power; and those in whom passion is strong, or who are not scrupulous, will assimilate the evil. Hence the Christian cannot consistently countenance the Theater. Here and there a brilliant young writer or preacher, a novelist or an utterer of startling paradoxes, may favor the Theater, but his observations on this and other subjects are as incapable of serious refutation as the incoherent ravings of frenzy. Such a minister is said to have declared that "to see a certain actor in tragedy has a better religious effect than an hour of prayer." These wild talkers soon come to pass at their proper worth, and though persons of sense may sometimes laugh with them, much oftener they laugh at them.

Some may try to impeach our statements of fact, but if the falsity of any assertion shall be shown, it will be promptly corrected. The utmost care cannot guarantee entire freedom from error. The propriety of furnishing an analysis of plays in an argument against the Theater may be doubted. But if so, it must be on the ground that some may be led to attend the Theater by reading the accounts of the plays. But if such a result were to follow, it would come either from a desire to see whether they have been correctly delineated, or from a wish to see the plays *if they are* as described. Little harm can be done in the latter case, for none who would really desire to see these plays if they are as stated, will be kept from the Theater by any arguments or influences whatever. In the former case the necessity does not exist. All these plays have been published by actors or for the use of actors, and if any one desires to see whether they are properly described he need not deceive himself by thinking that he must go to a Theater to do so. They can be procured and examined. The writer, however, has no fear that any who will take the trouble to do this will call his statements in question. Those who denounce him as inaccurate will be those who have never read the plays at all, and are comparing their partial recollection of what they heard with his description.

But to those who think it unwise to present the analysis, we wish to say that without this the argument would have no support. It would consist of naked assertions. To declare the Theater evil is not to prove it to be so, or to show why it is so. The Scriptures have not hesitated to describe sin for fear that some would be led by the vivid delineation of them to commit sins of which they were previously ignorant. But the Scriptures are not obnoxious to the charge of promoting sin. The purpose for which they portray it, the manner in which they do it, their uniform denunciation of it, and the tendency of their entire treatment of it, vindicate them from the charge. We know that we have not so described the plays analyzed as to make them attractive to any one whom we can hope to benefit.

Others may affirm that it is unjust to select objectionable plays and examine and condemn them by name, while the author admits that he found four or five which he approves, and does not give an analysis of these. To which he has to say, that when he began the examination, thrusting aside as far as possible his recollections, he carefully read nearly seventy plays. If the result had been that sixty were found unobjectionable, or only marred by inconsiderable defects, this argument would never have been written. If he had written any thing, it would have been in condemnation of the few and in praise of the many. But when, in the course of his reading, he became convinced that the number that could with propriety be enacted before youth, or read as they are acted, by a modest woman in a promiscuous company—that contain no disparaging allusions to religion, no profaneness, and nothing which tends to promote licentiousness, dissipation, or recklessness of life—is scarcely one in twelve; in a word, that the immense majority are such as have been described, and under that conviction he makes an argument *against the Thea-*

ter in *its relation to Christians and youth;* it is not pertinent to characterize those five or six further than to say they are unexceptionable. In a treatise expressly designed to warn people against settling in a malarious region, the author could hardly be expected to expatiate on the cheapness of a few building lots there, especially if *some were so anxious to reside in the infected district* that they would seize any pretext to justify it, and *even quote the friend who had warned* them against it as their *authority for going.*

There are others who think that a book against the Theater should abound in flaming appeals and solemn warnings. Certainly these have their place, but not in an argument. I have written to the judgment of ministers, teachers, parents, thoughtful men and women in every department of life, and to intelligent youth of both sexes. I can hardly expect a child to read or understand the train of thought herein pursued; but unless the average intelligence of youth is greatly overestimated, many such find pleasure in reading works addressed primarily to the understanding.

If, however, those who have read are convinced of the truth of the conclusion which is here maintained, whether they be ministers, parents, teachers, or friends, let *them*, strengthened by these or other, and, it may be, more convincing arguments, *make the appeals* for which their *personal* relations to those whom they address *prepare them.* If any who suppose the subject comparatively insignificant think that we have given it too much time, and displayed too much earnestness in its treatment, we ask them to consider whether the question be not vital to the evangelical Churches; whether, when Presbyterians, Congregationalists, Baptists, Methodists, and all others who maintain "the faith once delivered to the saints," generally attend the Theater, and *live in a manner corresponding* with the *state of conscience* and *religious feeling* which a love for the Theater as it now is and always has been, implies, revivals will not be unknown, conversions cease, and every form of worldliness overspread the Church.

Nothing can prevent the coming of such a period but the fidelity of ministers and Christians, especially in the great cities, and in wealthy Churches, where the tendency to patronize and apologize for the Theater is a symptom and fruit of that moral and spiritual enervation which thus far in the history of Christianity has been the concomitant, and, perhaps, the inevitable effect, of luxury.

THE END.

www.ingramcontent.com/pod-product-compliance
Lightning Source LLC
LaVergne TN
LVHW021405110826
845150LV00007B/1795

* 9 7 8 1 4 2 5 5 1 1 9 8 2 *